Contemplating
REALITY

Contemplating
REALITY

A PRACTITIONER'S GUIDE

TO THE VIEW IN

INDO-TIBETAN BUDDHISM

Andy Karr

SHAMBHALA
Boulder
2007

Shambhala Publications, Inc.
4720 Walnut Street
Boulder, Colorado 80301
www.shambhala.com

© 2007 by Andy Karr
Translations of twelve haiku on pages 64–66 from *The Essential Haiku: Versions of Bashō, Buson, and Issa,* edited and with an introduction by Robert Hass, copyright © 1994 by Robert Hass. Reprinted by permission of HarperCollins Publishers.

Illustration on page 90 from Robert Hooke's *Micrographia* reprinted by permission of Octavo Editions and the Warnock Library.

13 12 11 10 9 8 7 6 5

Printed in United States of America

⊗ This edition is printed on acid-free paper that meets the American National Standards Institute z39.48 Standard.

♻ Shambhala Publications makes every effort to print on recycled paper. For more information please visit www.shambhala.com.

Distributed in the United States by Penguin Random House LLC and in Canada by Random House of Canada Ltd

DESIGNED BY DEDE CUMMINGS DESIGNS

Library of Congress Cataloging-in-Publication Data

Karr, Andy.
Contemplating reality: a practitioner's guide to the view in Indo-Tibetan Buddhism/ Andy Karr.
p. cm.
Includes bibliographical references and index.
ISBN 978-1-59030-429-7 (alk. paper)
1. Buddhism–Doctrines. 2. Spiritual life—Buddhism. I. Title.
BQ4132.K376 2007
294.3'420423—dc22
2006035787

Homage

I pay homage to the Ocean of Dharma
I pay homage to the Ocean of Ethics
I pay homage to the Ocean of Qualities
And the oceans of compassionate ones who
    open the dharma gate.

By the merit of contemplating these teachings
May we penetrate the vital points of dharma
For the benefit of ourselves and others—
All sentient beings to the limits of space.

Contents

Foreword

BUDDHISM IS RICH WITH philosophical inquiry into the true nature of reality. The Buddha himself began this tradition by giving detailed presentations of a series of stages by which a person could gradually learn more and more about the actual nature of the universe, their own lives, and, most centrally, their own mind.

The learned Buddhist masters of India and the other countries to which Buddhism later spread then collected and wrote commentaries on these philosophical teachings the Buddha gave, in order to make them accessible to a wider audience.

Now it is wonderful that these teachings are making their way from east to west. Modern Westerners have the education and the inquisitive nature that make them perfect vessels to receive these teachings. They can receive these explanations in all their profundity and use them to analyze reality with all the rigor necessary to gain insight and wisdom.

For this to go well, it is essential that these teachings be presented clearly. To this end, I am delighted that Andy Karr, a learned student of both Chögyam Trungpa Rinpoche and my own root guru, Khenpo Tsültrim Gyamtso Rinpoche, has written this book that so clearly introduces the main points of Buddhist philosophical inquiry and the key methods for how to contemplate them and gain certainty in them. For no matter how profound and beneficial the teachings are, it is only when we have certainty in them that they will be of direct and immediate benefit to us personally.

Andy has taken great care in this book to guide new students on this path of contemplation and gaining certainty in reality's profound true nature. I pray that all who read this book will find it beneficial to their spiritual journey and that they will have the enthusiasm and confidence to proceed on this inner path of profound contemplation. The Buddha had the great confidence in human beings to present to them these most profound teachings and, in particular, modern Westerners are perfectly capable of understanding them and putting them into practice. May everyone do so, for the immeasurable benefit of sentient beings, who extend as far as the limits of space.

—DZOGCHEN PONLOP

Preface

THE GOAL OF THE BUDDHIST path is to transform ourselves into what we have always been. Rather than strive to become something better, which is ego's game, we learn to remove the mask of ego to reveal our true nature. The method for doing this is to listen to the dharma, to reflect on its meaning, and to meditate within the inquisitiveness and understanding that these produce.

This process of transformation does not occur through acquiring lots of knowledge or perfecting sophisticated meditation techniques. It occurs through seeing through delusion and letting go of fixation. Contemplation and investigation play an essential role in this process, one that is easily overlooked. Today, there is much written about the teachings of Buddhism and much written about the practice of meditation. This book focuses on contemplation, which makes a link between these two. I have written it because after years of practicing the dharma, contemplation brought out my own inquisitiveness and refreshed my attitude toward the journey, and I have seen it do the same for many dharma friends.

Some people are attracted to Buddhism because of teachings that clarify the nature of reality. Others are attracted by the practices of meditation that transform the mind. Still others by Buddhism's ideal of universal compassion and its systems of ethics that help navigate the challenges of life and death. Human beings have both minds and hearts—intellect and insight. Liberation is quite a difficult undertaking, and one of the greatest challenges of the spiritual journey is to bring intellect and insight together to travel the path. Buddhism is blessed with extremely rich scholarly traditions for developing intellect, and extremely rich practice traditions for developing experience and insight, but it is often difficult for practitioners to bring them together. Sometimes practice and study seem to speak different languages. Our own deep-rooted tendencies may also draw us toward one and repel us from the other.

It is said that studying the dharma without meditating is like trying to scale a rock face with no arms, while practicing meditation without studying is like trying to make a long journey without eyes. Contemplation is the bridge between intellect and insight, study and meditation. To bring all our resources to bear on the journey, we need to join the practices of study, contemplation, and meditation together like three strong locomotives pulling the train of our delusion to the destination of realization.

What is contemplation? It is mixing the teachings with our experience. Contemplation is a bridge to study for meditators because it arouses inquisitiveness about the nature of meditation and postmeditation experience. Reflecting on the meaning and implications of the teachings puts meditation in a larger perspective than simply cultivating what we believe to be wholesome states of mind or trying to master a series of techniques. Study and contemplation arouse insight and give meditation direction and focus. Insight and focus make meditation an effective means of transformation.

For the scholarly, contemplation is a bridge to meditation because it takes intellectual understanding and joins it with experience. Reflecting on the teachings means leaving the purely conceptual and discursive for the experiential. This naturally connects us to the practice of meditation if we are to pursue the investigation. In this way, conceptual understanding is transformed into experience and realization.

My Buddhist journey began sometime in the winter of 1970 when I visited a small *zendo* in New York City. I had gotten it into my head that I wanted to become a Zen master (probably from reading *Zen in the Art of Archery* as a teenager, and watching too many Toshiro Mifune samurai movies). As I recall, there didn't seem to be much going on at the zendo, but I did find a pamphlet for Shunryu Suzuki Roshi's recently published *Zen Mind, Beginner's Mind*. That little sampling of Suzuki Roshi's language and imagery hooked me, and a couple of days later I picked up a copy of the book at the New Yorker bookstore on the Upper West Side.

Soon afterward, I borrowed a friend's copy of Chögyam Trungpa's early autobiography, *Born in Tibet*, and followed that up with his first book of teachings in the West, *Meditation in Action*. By the following September I had dropped out of Columbia University and moved to San Francisco to practice Zen. A few months later Suzuki Roshi died, and I moved on to Boulder, Colorado, to study with Trungpa Rinpoche, who became my root teacher.

Trungpa Rinpoche expected his students to meditate a lot. He often said that we could not understand what he taught if we didn't practice enough. People kept practice records that he personally reviewed. After several years of basic training, students attended the three-month Vajradhatu Seminary, where intense periods of practice and study alternated, along with a healthy dose of work and ordinary activity. During the seventeen years Trungpa Rinpoche taught in North America, he conducted thirteen seminaries to give students a comprehensive overview of the Buddhist teachings. He taught the stages of the view, which represent progressively more subtle ways of understanding reality; the progression of meditation methods that students work with as they journey along the path; the stages of conduct that bring view and meditation into daily life; and the stages of realization that constitute the path itself.

After seminary, students embarked on vajrayana training, which included further study and practice. Trungpa Rinpoche created the Nalanda Translation Committee to produce practice liturgies in accessible English as well as extensive practice manuals with instructions on procedures and teachings on view. He conducted numerous Vajra Assemblies to teach vajrayana view and practice. He created Naropa Institute (now Naropa University) to join meditation practice with Western scholarship and create a true contemplative education. Even the experiential Shambhala Training curriculum culminated in an intensive study program. The message was clear: practice and study went together like two wings of a bird.

After Trungpa Rinpoche's passing in 1987, his students soldiered on. In the early 1990s some of us began to study with the yogi-scholar Khenpo Tsültrim Gyamtso Rinpoche. Although very different from Trungpa Rinpoche in style, his profundity, outrageousness, and commitment to working with Westerners were the same. Khenpo Rinpoche presented the most profound dharma in a completely experiential way. In his youth in eastern Tibet, he trained with many masters, wandering from place to place, studying the life and songs of the great yogi Milarepa and practicing meditation in solitary caves and charnel grounds. When the Chinese took over in 1959, he led a group of nuns and laypeople across the Himalayas to safety in India.

Following his escape from Tibet, Khenpo Rinpoche joined the path of scholarship to his yogic realization. He spent nine years studying and mastering the sutras and tantras at a monastic university in India, which the Dalai Lama named *Listening and Reflecting for Those Who Desire Liberation.*

At the direction of the sixteenth Gyalwang Karmapa (head of the Kagyu lineage—one of four Tibetan Buddhist lineages), Khenpo Rinpoche started to teach in the West in 1977. Since then he has circled the globe thirteen times, working with students throughout Europe, North America, South America, Asia, and Australasia. In 1985 he had a brief meeting with Trungpa Rinpoche at the Kalapa Court in Boulder. Afterward, Trungpa Rinpoche remarked approvingly to a friend that Khenpo Rinpoche was "more yogi than khenpo." Within a year of first hearing Khenpo Rinpoche teach, I discovered I had a second root teacher.

It is difficult to generalize about Khenpo Rinpoche's methods of working with students. They are individual and quite varied. However, basic training usually consists of extensive study of the progressive stages of the view, accompanied by practice of progressive stages of meditation and conduct, to transform view into experience.

There are countless ways to train students in the Buddhist tradition. In general, accumulating a good foundation of knowledge and method is necessary. However, accumulating intellectual understanding and practice techniques are not ends in themselves. To progress beyond the initial stages of the path we need to develop insight. Ultimately, to win success on the path, wisdom must dawn from within.

For insight to develop and for wisdom to dawn, we need to be inquisitive about the nature of our world, our experience, and our minds. With inquisitiveness, both practice and study are fresh and exciting. Contemplation is a method for bringing out our inquisitiveness and creating a bridge between study and practice; it can transform our attitude about the path from dutiful to joyful. While there will always be difficult stretches and frustrations on the path, inquisitiveness transforms an arduous journey into a voyage of discovery.

Notes about Translated Material

I CONSIDERED EDITING or paraphrasing the translated material in the book to make it more accessible, but in the end, resisted the temptation. Since this book is about contemplation, I think you will discover that you can unpack even the more opaque translations just by contemplating them. That is an important skill to develop.

On the other hand, I *have* modified some of the quotations by removing the brackets that translators sometimes use to show that they have added words or phrases that are implied in the original text rather than explicitly stated (this is particularly common in translations from Tibetan). Therefore, any brackets you see in the quotations will be my additions, not the translator's.

I have also included occasional Sanskrit or Tibetan words when I felt they were useful terms for people to know. In all cases, one or more English equivalents are also given. The foreign words are not transliterated using diacritical marks or formal systems of transliteration that would be found in scholarly presentations, but are written so that the uninitiated English speaker can pronounce them approximately like the originals.

Contemplating
REALITY

1

ROPES AND SNAKES

IMAGINE IT IS TWILIGHT AND you are walking alone in a forest. As the light fades, you can't see very well. You come upon a long, thin shape on the path. You are startled and then begin to feel afraid. It's a snake! But wait. Something is not quite right. It's not moving. You are not really sure what it is. You pluck up your courage and move closer. You poke it with a stick, and it still doesn't move. You pick it up with the stick and find that it is just a striped piece of rope. Your fear evaporates. How could you possibly be afraid of an old piece of rope? How silly.

The snake that is only a rope is a classical Buddhist illustration of ignorance. Ironically, the most basic teachings of the Buddha are not about attaining the glories of enlightenment or nirvana. They are about ignorance: not knowing who we really are or what we really are. In Sanskrit the term for ignorance is *avidya. Vidya* is "knowing" and *a* makes it negative, so "not knowing." Tibetans translated this as *marikpa. Rikpa* is "awareness or knowing," and again *ma* makes it negative—"unawareness."

Ignorance is the root of samsara, the suffering of cyclic existence. Because we don't know the true nature of our existence, we suffer. Simply put, the core of our ignorance is that we don't know that "I" and "mine" don't truly exist. We think they do. We think and talk about them all the time, but in fact they are just like illusions and dreams. The "self," or "ego," is like the snake that is really an old piece of rope. When we truly see that the self does not exist, we stop clinging to it, just as we stop mistaking the rope for a snake. When our self-clinging dissolves, all suffering based on the self dissolves as well, like the fear of the snake. This is what the Buddha taught.

Movies can illustrate the same thing. Once the interminable previews and advertisements finish and the feature starts to roll, what happens? If the movie is good, we get totally engrossed. We lose track of the fact that we are sitting in a movie theater watching light projected on a screen. It feels like we are looking at real people and places. If the story gets scary, we feel fear. Unless we remind ourselves, "This is only a movie," that fear can get intense. When a well-made film gets scary, I try to remember it is just a movie and that I am sitting in a theater. That works for about half a minute. Usually I get sucked in again instantly. It is only when the credits roll and the lights come up that the illusion dissipates, and with it the emotionality. If the movie is a comedy, the illusion can make us happy, yet that happiness also dissolves when the movie ends. The Buddha taught that our lives are as illusory as a movie.

Because we take "I" and "mine" as real, even though they are illusions, we ride an emotional roller coaster, needlessly and endlessly. We are constantly tossed about by hope and fear: hope that "I" will get what it wants, and fear that "I" will lose what it has, get what it doesn't want, and in the end, experience the misery of old age, sickness, and death. The Buddha described these phenomena as the truths of suffering and its cause. The first truth is the pervasiveness of suffering; the second truth is that the cause of this pervasive suffering is clinging to the illusions of "I" and "mine" as though they were real.

This is summarized nicely by a quote from the seventh-century Indian Buddhist master Dharmakirti:*

When there is self, one believes there is other,
From these images of self and other come attachment
    and aversion,
As a result of getting wrapped up in these,
All possible faults arise.[1]

As an aside, since this book is about contemplation, you will find lots of quotations from great scholars and practitioners in it. These quotations make pithy contemplations that express the dharma in clear and concise ways. They also contain blessings because they come from holders of the Buddha's lineage who directly realized the true meaning, just as it is, beyond inference or intellectual speculation.

THE OTHER TRUTHS

The Buddha's teachings would not have spread very far if he had only described suffering and the cause of suffering. Fortunately, he also explained cessation of suffering and its cause, and he did it so well that we are still practicing his teachings 2,500 years later.

Different Buddhist traditions have different ways of understanding the cessation of suffering and the methods for bringing it about. A basic presentation of cessation that is in harmony with the explanations of most traditions is that cessation is caused by directly seeing selflessness, egolessness, or emptiness (*selflessness* and *egolessness* are different translations of the same Sanskrit word). To go back to our illustrations, cessation comes about

---

* Appendix 1 gives brief biographies of Dharmakirti and other major Buddhist historical figures.

from seeing that the snake is just a rope, or that the people in the movie are just images projected on a screen. There never was a snake on the path or people in the movie. That does not mean that there was nothing there. There was a striped rope that was mistaken for a snake, and light reflecting from the screen that was mistaken for places and people. What ceases is mistaking them for what they are not.

In the same way, there has never truly been a self, and our projections never truly existed. The vast variety of appearances that we normally take to be real exist merely as appearances. With cessation we recognize them for what they are. We recognize what is called their "suchness," which means we see them as they really are.

Khenpo Tsültrim Gyamtso explains this by saying, "Samsara is like making a mistake, and nirvana is like when you stop making it." Khenpo Tsültrim often illustrates this transformation with the analogy of recognizing a dream to be a dream while you are dreaming. When you stop making the mistake of taking the dream to be real, the dream images do not cease, but your confusion about them does.

To summarize cessation, we could take the verse from Dharmakirti presenting the result of believing in a self and restate it to show what happens when the absence of self is recognized:

When there is no self, what can be known as other?
Therefore there is no attachment or aversion
By becoming familiar with this,
Peace arises.

OVERCOMING IGNORANCE

We have been discussing what is called "the view," the basic Buddhist understanding of reality. In particular, we have been discussing the view of egolessness or selflessness. Having briefly discussed the view, we can begin to talk about the remedy for mistakenness.

The way to overcome unawareness, or not knowing, is through awareness, or knowing. This knowing is not something that anyone else can give us, like the answers to a math test. We won't find it on the Internet. What we need is to develop the intelligence or insight that sees through the mistake or the illusion. This intelligence or insight is called *prajna* in Sanskrit and *sherap* in Tibetan.

This prajna already exists within us, but we need to cultivate it to bring it out. To do this, we need inquisitiveness. If we are not inquisitive about egolessness and genuine reality, if we go on thinking, "I am real and this world is real, so what's the point of all this Buddhist hoo-ha?" nothing is going to happen. We can't just freeze forever in the face of the snake. We need to poke at it and find out what it really is.

To do this, we need to use three activities or methods: *listening* to the teachings on genuine reality, *contemplating* these teachings, and *meditating*. Sometimes we talk of three types of prajna that arise from these three activities: the prajna that comes from listening, the prajna that comes from contemplating, and the prajna that comes from meditating.

Here is the way this logic is presented by the great nineteenth-century scholar-yogi Jamgön Kongtrul Lodrö Thayé in *The Treasury of Knowledge*, one of his *Five Great Treasuries* that encompass the depth and breadth of the Buddhist teachings as they were known in the Tibet of his time. (We will hear quite a bit more from Jamgön Kongtrul as we progress through this book.) First he explains that to attain nirvana, or deathlessness, we need the prajna that eliminates ignorance:

What one strives for is nirvana, a place without death.
This will not arise without prajna, the remedy for
    eliminating ignorance,

The root of obscuration. Through prajna, pure view is
    attained.
Through skilful means, pure conduct is attained.
Through uniting completely pure view and conduct,
    liberation is swiftly attained.[2]

Next he explains that eliminating belief in the self, or the ego,
is the key to liberation, and it is prajna that realizes selflessness,
or egolessness; that is why we need to train in the three activities
that give rise to prajna:

> If you do not eradicate the view of a self along with its seed,
> there is no way to attain liberation from the three realms.
> If there is no prajna to realize no-self, you cannot give up
> the view of a self. Therefore, you train in the completely
> pure view through the three activities of listening, reflect-
> ing and meditating. And in this way you should give rise to
> flawless prajna.[3]

LISTENING

Listening means listening to teachings as well as studying them
on our own. The prajna that arises from this is easy to understand: through listening to and studying the dharma we develop
a general understanding of the way things are. This corrects our
most coarse misunderstandings about reality.

There are things to cultivate when you listen or study, as well
as things to avoid. When you listen or study, at the beginning, it
helps to rouse your enthusiasm and alertness. You don't need to
make a big deal of this, but you can make an effort to brighten
your awareness and interest. Sometimes it helps to remember
that the teachings are beneficial to you and might be beneficial
to others if you take them to heart. Sometimes you will have
trouble following a teaching, or get drowsy and start to lose track

of what you are hearing or studying. Don't get agitated. Tuning in to sights and sounds in the environment will help you settle down.

When you listen and study, try to understand both the logic and how the different topics connect. The most important thing is to "use your antennae," as Chögyam Trungpa Rinpoche often admonished students. You don't need to depend on discursive mind alone to understand the dharma.

The things to avoid can be hard to spot since they are often part of our habitual style and seem quite natural, or perhaps even "virtuous." (This is similar to the way we don't notice the smell of our own bodies).

- Don't listen or study *like a politician*, clinging to your point of view or some party line. Who cares if you have studied great teachings in the past? What's the point of studying the dharma for self-confirmation? As the great Indian teacher Atisha said, "The best spiritual friend is one who attacks your hidden faults. The best instructions are the ones that hit those faults."
- Don't listen or study *like a movie critic*, evaluating the language and style of the teacher rather than listening to the substance of what he or she teaches. You might be able to amuse your friends with some sharp criticism later on, but in the end you will pay a price.
- Don't listen or study *like a consumer*, picking and choosing among teachings and teachers the way you would choose detergent in the supermarket. All of the Buddha's teachings present the truth and are worth studying and understanding. You might not know the value of a particular teaching at the time you hear it, but ten or twenty years from now, it might provide you with a critical piece of the puzzle.
- Don't listen or study *like an orphan*, feeling too pathetic to be able to understand what is being taught. The dharma is about

you, not some obscure points in calculus, so if you keep working at it, you will definitely understand.

* Don't listen or study *like a "dharma groupie,"* so infatuated with the messenger that you never get the message.

CONTEMPLATING

The second method for arousing prajna is contemplating; in fact, contemplating is the main subject of this book. Most of us approach Buddhism with a certain respect for meditation, and an appreciation for studying the teachings. On the other hand, the importance of contemplation might be less obvious. It is an essential activity, yet one that is often overlooked.

Contemplation reveals our own intelligence to us, often in surprising ways. Profound teachings can clarify themselves simply through the process of repeated examination. What at first is unclear becomes clear. Details that we've overlooked jump out at us. You might think that you can't understand something, but by contemplating it you find that you can understand. With contemplation, you can understand the implications of the material, not just what is actually said.

We have all experienced reading or hearing teachings, understanding something for a moment, and then discovering later that it's gone. Sometimes parts of the teaching are not clear and we skip over them. Profound teachings don't really penetrate until you make them part of your personal experience—take them in, chew on them, reflect on them, ask yourself, "Is this true?" "Do I experience it this way?" "What is the point of this teaching?"

Thinking about the teachings in this way may seem to contradict the emphasis on "nonconceptuality" found in many Buddhist instructions, but there is no contradiction. We need to use thought to get beyond thought. Real nonconceptuality arises from recognizing the true nature of conceptuality, not through blocking thoughts or getting rid of them.

We need to reflect on the teachings a great deal, particularly the teachings on egolessness—which are so profound and subtle—so that they become part of our basic understanding. Through this process, we gradually develop certainty about the way things really are. Having this certainty, genuine nonconceptual understanding will arise during the third activity: meditating.

Khenpo Tsültrim describes the need for contemplating emptiness in *Ascertaining Certainty About the View*:

> The purpose of contemplating the teachings . . . is to develop certainty about what the meaning of emptiness really is. You have doubts, for example, and by working with those doubts you come to a kind of clarity when they disappear. It may take some time to see, "I do not really understand this" or "I'm not sure of this." So you examine these doubts, these places where it seems foggy. And gradually, you come to a really clear picture for yourself of what emptiness is. Then with the clear conviction, "This is emptiness," you meditate, resting within that certainty. You meditate settled into the conviction that you have generated through reflecting on the meaning of emptiness.[4]

MEDITATING

Through contemplation we develop certainty in egolessness, but this is still an intellectual understanding. Without meditation, we don't experience egolessness directly. Without direct experience of egolessness, we continue to feel that "I" and "mine" exist, and keep wandering in samsara, fooled by our own projections. As the omniscient Jigme Lingpa said, "Theory is like a patch on a coat—one day it will come apart." That's why we need to meditate within the understanding we have developed through listening and contemplating.

This is how Dzogchen Patrul Rinpoche describes the way understanding is transformed into realization through the practice of meditation in *Words of My Perfect Teacher*:

Through meditation, as you gain practical experience of what you have understood intellectually, the true realization of the natural state develops in you without any mistake. Certainty is born from within. Liberated from confining doubts and hesitations, you see the very face of the natural state.

Having first eliminated all your doubts through hearing and reflection, you come to the practical experience of meditation, and see everything as empty forms without any substantiality, as in the eight similes of illusion:

As in a dream, all the external objects perceived with the five senses are not there, but appear through delusion.

As in a magic show, things are made to appear by a temporary conjunction, circumstances and connections.

As in a visual aberration, things appear to be there, yet there is nothing.

As in a mirage, things appear but are not real.

As in an echo, things can be perceived but there is nothing there, either outside or inside.

As in a city of gandharvas,* there is neither a dwelling nor anyone to dwell.

As in a reflection, things appear but have no reality of their own.

As in a city created by magic, there are all sorts of appearances but they are not really there.

Seeing all the objects of your perception in this way, you come to understand that all these appearances are

---

* Literally *gandharva* means "smell eater." They are mythical beings who seem to disappear as you get close to them.

false by their very nature. When you look into the nature of the subject that perceives them—the mind—those objects that appear to it do not stop appearing, but the concepts that take them as having any true existence subside. To leave the mind in the realization of the nature of reality, empty yet clear like the sky, is transcendent wisdom.[5]

Meditation is a vast subject, and there are limitless numbers of meditation techniques. For now, we will look at some of the basic principles. There are two main aspects to the practice of meditation: cultivating peace and cultivating insight. Cultivating peace, called *shamatha* in Sanskrit and *shi-ne* in Tibetan, is learning to let the mind come to rest. Cultivating insight, called *vipashyana* in Sanskrit and *lhagthong* in Tibetan, is learning to recognize the nature of phenomena and the nature of the mind. To develop the prajna that comes from meditating, we need to work with both shamatha and vipashyana.

Most of us experience constant cascades of thoughts, emotions, and mental images, like overlapping waves on the sea or billowing clouds in the sky. It is hard to recognize anything in this murky mass of activity. Before insight can develop, we need to let mind settle and clarify itself. Basically, this aspect of meditation is learning to work with the energy of mind rather than struggling against it.

Once you get a little experience of peace, it feels quite satisfying. You might think, "I have really accomplished something. This is what meditation is all about!" It is tempting to think that shamatha is all we need to solve our problems, and easy to get ambitious about cultivating peace. However, this type of meditation only produces temporary relief. Experience shows that no matter how good we get at settling our minds, sooner or later we again have to deal with our thoughts, emotions, and mental images. That is why we don't need to worry about getting rid of them. Without them, there will be nothing to work with to cultivate insight, since it is recognizing the true nature of thoughts, emotions, and mental images that provides permanent relief—just as recognizing the snake to be a rope, the movie to be mere images projected on a screen, and the dream to be a dream are the only things are that provide real relief.

There are different ways to cultivate insight. Sometimes we need to vigorously investigate or analyze our experience, asking ourselves questions that come from our contemplations. We might ask such questions as "Is the body the self, or is the mind?" or "What is 'the thinker' like?" At other times, we need to let go of investigating and analyzing and rest in our natural wakefulness or panoramic awareness.

The key point in meditation is balance. We need to develop a feeling for when to rest the mind, when to investigate and analyze, and when to cultivate nonconceptual inquisitiveness. Meditation is as much "art" as it is "science." Just as in painting or music, we need to do a lot of practice to become artful.

To summarize the three prajnas, here is another quotation from Jamgön Kongtrul, this time from his verse overview of the vajrayana path called *Creation and Completion:*

It is as the noble Nagarjuna said:

> Listening to Dharma engenders contemplation,
> and contemplation gives rise to the meditation
>   experience—this is the sequence.
> So if you abandon distraction and continuously apply
>   effort,
> first the prajna that comes from listening
> will result in comprehension of the general
>   characteristics of the dharmas of samsara and
>   nirvana.
> Then, contemplation will pacify blatant grasping to
>   the reality of illusory appearances,

meditation develops the definitive direct experience of mind, and so on.

Thus the previous stages act as causes for the arising of the latter.

When this is not the case, it is like desiring results without any cause.[6]

2

MAKING THE JOURNEY

LIKE MISTAKING A NEW job in a dream for a real career move, we mistake what isn't a self to be a self, and our projections to be real objects. You could say that sorting out this confusion is the central koan of this book. To solve this koan, we need to make a journey of exploration and discovery. It is not enough to just think, "There is no self" or "Everything is empty." If we don't *see* what it is that we mistake to be a self, and what it is we mistake to be real objects, we will not be freed from delusion and suffering— just as we are forced to ride the roller coaster of happiness and sorrow in a dream until we see that the dream job is made out of dream-stuff.

There are lots of contemplations and investigations in this book to help us awaken the prajna that sees through delusion. As you go through these contemplations, from time to time ask yourself, "What do I mistake to be 'me'?" "What do I mistake to be 'real things'?" It is not easy to deal with such basic questions, and you need to work at it slowly and patiently. We have tremendous emotional resistance to recognizing egolessness. There is great security in the familiar ground of "me" and "my projections." Even if you feel that your life is a misery, it is "your misery." In contrast, the openness of selflessness feels groundless and frightening at first. That's why you need to approach it gradually until you start to realize that you are not losing anything except your delusions.

To contemplate egolessness, you need to ask yourself a lot of questions. This is the way to provoke prajna. In the beginning these questions might seem quite stupid. At times it feels like you are about to see something, but then your mind veers off, like a pilot making touch-and-go landings or a rock skimming on a pond. Sometimes you catch a glimpse, and then your excitement covers over what you saw. Sometimes nothing seems to happen at all. That's the way these investigations proceed. Here is another quote from Khenpo Tsültrim's *Ascertaining Certainty About the View*:

> In Buddhism, you are encouraged to use your own intelligence to analyze whatever is happening; you analyze yourself or the various views. Not only are you allowed, but you are encouraged to do this. The metaphor that is used to illustrate this is the purchase of gold. Before you bought it, you would examine it well before you paid out so much money. In the same way, you use your prajna to analyze and to examine the situation well. There are many different stages of analysis within the different vehicles and also within the different views. What is this self? What are phenomena? These are questions that scholars and the realized masters of the past asked themselves over and over again. They found answers to those questions, which were then included within the treatises. There is probably no rock that they did not overturn, no kind of questioning they did not pursue.[1]

Why do we find it difficult to investigate and analyze? Because ego has tremendous resources to fend off anything that might expose its basic duplicity and remove its security. You can learn a lot about this from Chögyam Trungpa's brilliant *Cutting*

Through Spiritual Materialism, in which he explains in detail ego's need for material, psychological, and spiritual comforts and security. He shows how ingenious ego is in maintaining the illusion of a solid, continuous self, and that unmasking ego is the heart of the spiritual journey, which ego continually tries to subvert and sidetrack.

Gradual and Sudden Paths

You might wonder if everyone has to go through a gradual path of awakening, or if sudden enlightenment is possible. These different types of realization occur for different types of students. The students of greatest capacity are the *sudden types,* who, simply upon hearing about selflessness or the nature of mind, recognize the true nature of reality, just as it is. Students of a middle level of capacity are called *alternators*—sometimes they get it, and sometimes they don't. The students of lesser capacities are the *gradual types,* who need to slowly and systematically go through the stages of the path.

Unfortunately, most of us fall into this last category, but there is no reason we need to feel cheated. It is said that the reason students are of different capacity is because they have done different amounts of listening, contemplating, and meditating in previous lives, and bring more or less delusion with them to this life. The sudden types are people who have gained great realization in the past and just need to be reminded to look in order to see things as they truly are.

When people of lesser capacity hear about sudden realization, it can give them a "silver bullet" mentality. For years, I practiced and studied, hoping that sudden enlightenment would strike. I guess it was better than not practicing and studying and hoping that sudden enlightenment would strike, but it was still pretty naive. All that hope and fear just obscures the prajna that sees through delusion.

Shunryu Suzuki explains gradual realization in *Zen Mind, Beginner's Mind* in the following way:

> After you have practiced for a while, you will realize that it is not possible to make rapid, extraordinary progress. Even though you try very hard, the progress you make is always little by little. It is not like going out in a shower in which you know when you get wet. In a fog, you do not know you are getting wet, but as you keep walking you get wet little by little. If your mind has ideas of progress, you may say, "Oh, this pace is terrible!" But actually it is not. When you get wet in a fog it is very difficult to dry yourself.[2]

Teachings on sudden enlightenment versus teachings on the gradual path are just one of many seemingly contradictory presentations we come upon as we travel on the path. One of the more difficult aspects of making the journey is understanding how teachings presented from different viewpoints can be integrated. To do this, we need an overview of the terrain we are traveling on. There are many different presentations of what this terrain is like, just as geographical maps can be drawn to show political boundaries, topography, transportation networks, or other features of an area. Here are two relevant presentations of the geography of the path.

The Three Dharmachakras

Although the three *dharmachakras*, or three turnings of the wheel of dharma, are often presented as the historical evolution of the teachings, they also provide a framework for understanding the main stages of the path.

Sentient beings need to be led to the truth in stages, because if someone tried to present the most profound reality all at once, either they wouldn't have a clue what the person was talking about, or they would think the teacher was nuts! It is not easy to recognize a dream while you are dreaming, or a rope/snake while you are terrified. Certainly, it is not easy to recognize selflessness and emptiness when you are deeply habituated and attached to the self and to your projections.

If someone had an intense snake phobia, it wouldn't do a lot of good to tell them to go pick up the rope/snake. "Pick up that snake? You must be kidding!" First you would need to desensitize them by explaining that while some snakes are poisonous, most are harmless and even helpful: they keep down rodent populations, they do not see humans as food, they do not strike unless they feel threatened. You would show them pictures of snakes and eventually have them handle rubber snakes. Then you might give them special instructions and tools for handling snakes safely. By that time, they might be ready to go check out our illusory friend.

In the same way, sentient beings have intense egolessness phobia. To help us overcome this, the Buddha introduced the true nature of reality in stages. The *first-turning teachings* are presented in terms of the way things appear to ordinary beings. The self exists. Things exist. The world exists. Sentient beings exist. The three times (past, present, and future) exist. Suffering exists. Cessation of suffering exists. The path that brings cessation of suffering exists. This is what is called apparent reality. It is the way reality appears to deluded beings, and it is in these terms that the teachings of the first turning are presented.

In this context, the Buddha taught that all positive states of existence arise from virtuous deeds. All negative states of existence arise from nonvirtuous deeds. Liberation arises from removing obscurations from body and mind. He taught that all dharmas (phenomena) are marked with impermanence, selflessness, and suffering and that only nirvana is peace. In short, he taught how cause and effect work at the level of apparent reality.

The second- and third-turning teachings are not presented from the point of view of the way things ordinarily appear but from the way they actually are. This is called "genuine reality." Once students begin to wear out their attachment to delusion through following the teachings of the first turning, they are able to hear the teachings of the second turning. The *second-turning teachings* present essencelessness, or *shunyata*—that all phenomena are empty of true existence, like dreams.

The quintessential second-turning teaching is the *Sutra of the Heart of Transcendent Knowledge* ("transcendent knowledge" is a translation of the Sanskrit term *prajnaparamita*), often referred to simply as the Heart Sutra. Here is a section of that sutra as translated by the Nalanda Translation Committee:

O Shariputra, a son or daughter of noble family who wishes to practice the profound prajnaparamita should see in this way: seeing the five skandhas to be empty of nature. Form is emptiness; emptiness also is form. Emptiness is no other than form; form is no other than emptiness. In the same way, feeling, perception, formation, and consciousness are emptiness. Thus Shariputra, all dharmas are emptiness. There are no characteristics. There is no birth and no cessation. There is no impurity and no purity. There is no decrease and no increase. Therefore, Shariputra, in emptiness, there is no form, no feeling, no perception, no formation, no consciousness; no eye, no ear, no nose, no tongue, no body, no mind; no appearance, no sound, no smell, no taste, no touch, no dharmas; no eye dhatu up to no mind dhatu, no dhatu of dharmas, no mind consciousness dhatu; no ignorance, no end of ignorance up to no old age and death, no end of old age and death; no suffering, no origin of suffering, no cessation of suffering, no path, no wisdom, no attainment, and no nonattainment. Therefore, Shariputra, since the bodhisattvas have no attainment, they abide by means of prajnaparamita. Since there is no obscuration of mind, there is no fear. They transcend falsity and attain complete nirvana.[3]

All phenomena are emptiness—while they appear, they are empty. While they are empty, they appear. The "falsity" that bodhisattvas transcend is the same as the mistakenness that we have been discussing.

The teachings of the third turning explain that all dharmas are the play of original wisdom or radiant clarity. This is the *tathagata-garbha*, or buddha nature. In ordinary beings, this wisdom is obscured by temporary stains of conceptuality and emotionality arising from our mistakenness. In buddhas, this wisdom is fully revealed. A metaphor for the way buddha nature is present in ordinary sentient beings is the sun when it is obscured by clouds. The sun is always shining. The clouds are temporary obscurations. When the clouds are blown away by the wind, the sun's radiance is clearly visible.

The following verse from the *Mahayana Uttaratantra-shastra* describes the way buddha nature is present in sentient beings:

The Buddha has said that all beings have buddha nature
"since buddha wisdom is always present within the
     assembly of beings,
since this undefiled nature is free from duality,
and since the disposition to buddhahood has been named
     after its fruit."[4]

Khenpo Tsültrim's special explanation of the three dharmachakras is that the first-turning teachings present *the truth of apparent reality.* The second-turning teachings refute *what genuine reality is not,* and the third-turning teachings assert *what genuine reality is.*

The teachings of the various turnings are complementary and

not contradictory. Until we have attained complete realization, we need to work with all three. The first-turning teachings are particularly helpful in guiding our understanding of conduct and karmic results. The second-turning teachings are particularly helpful when we are clarifying our understanding of the profound view. The third-turning teachings are particularly helpful for developing profound meditation.

The Stages of Investigation

Another map of the Buddhist journey is called "the stages of meditation on emptiness" or "the stages of prajna meditation." This is a sequence of investigations that strip away the conceptual and emotional veils from samsara to reveal its genuine nature— nirvana. The investigations proceed from coarse to more and more subtle, and roughly parallel the historical evolution of Buddhist traditions in India.

In the first centuries of the Common Era,* Indian Buddhism flourished and evolved rapidly. Nagarjuna and Asanga and their followers produced a great ocean of mahayana teachings. As far as we know, these teachers did not see themselves belonging to separate schools, but later scholars, looking back at their exuberant outpouring and the teachings of the earlier traditions, organized them into a framework of schools and subschools as pedagogical tools. To differentiate the schools, they identified different systems of tenets.

These tenets are often called philosophical systems, but they are a little different from philosophical systems as we know them in the West. The systems are not elaborated as ends in themselves but rather with the pragmatic intention of aiding practitioners in

---

* The Common Era (C.E.) is the period beginning with the year one in the Gregorian calendar, and is equivalent to *anno Domini* (A.D.), but without the Christian overtones.

their quest for liberation. Buddhist tenets indicate ways of investigating reality directly, through the practices of contemplation and meditation.

The systems of tenets are more like theoretical work in science than philosophical projects. A scientific theory describes a certain understanding of phenomena and indicates fruitful areas for new exploration and experimentation. Likewise, the tenets describe the relationship of apparent reality to genuine reality, and indicate how to investigate these realities.

Another way of describing the role of tenets is to think about the traditional image of the teachings being like a finger pointing at the moon. Think of tenets as progressively more subtle and accurate gestures that guide us toward directly seeing things as they are. First, the illuminated landscape of a moonlit night might be pointed out. Next, we might be shown glowing clouds in a certain portion of the sky. Then the moon's radiance might be indicated. Finally, the glowing disk itself could be pointed out. In this way we are gradually led to see what is subtle and profound.

The different stages of meditation on emptiness are named after the schools of tenets that the investigations are based on (see table).

THE SCHOOLS OF TENETS

Vaibhashika, or Particularist, School

Sautrantika, or Followers of Sutra, School

Chittamatra, or Mind Only, School

Madhyamaka, or Middle Way, Schools
  • Rangtong, or Self-Empty, Schools
    — Svatantrika, or Autonomy, School
    — Prasangika, or Consequence, School
  • Shentong, or Empty-of-Other, School

The sequence of investigations provides a general framework for the contemplations in the remainder of this book. What follows is a brief outline of the stages. Don't worry about getting all the names and details. They will be developed in greater detail as we go along, and there is a chart to refer to in appendix 2.

The first stage is named after the Vaibhashika school. One etymology of the word *vaibhashika* can be translated as "particularist." The name comes from this school's emphasis on the fragmentary nature of reality. The investigations use subtle impermanence to analyze experience and reveal that which is ultimately real. They say that only the most minute particles of matter and most subtle moments of consciousness are genuinely real. Coarse things and durations of consciousness that appear don't truly exist: they are just concepts and labels superimposed onto collections of these partless particles and moments of mind.

The next stage is named after the Sautrantika school. *Sautrantika* means "followers of sutra." This school provides a different way of deconstructing the way things appear. They say that things that truly exist are things that can perform functions, such as the directly perceived objects of the five senses: sights, sounds, smells, tastes, and bodily sensations; as well as the consciousnesses that perceive them. What cannot perform a function does not truly exist; it is only a deceptive appearance. For example, the spoon that you directly perceive on your kitchen table is genuinely real, but it is not connected with any name or label—it is merely an object of your eye-sense-consciousness. On the other hand, the object that appears to your conceptual mind when you think "spoon" cannot hold any soup—it cannot perform a function, so it does not truly exist.

The next stage is named after the Chittamatra, or "Mind Only," school. This school says that dualistic appearances of perceived objects and perceiving subjects are deceptive. All outer and inner appearances are only mind. They use dreams as examples of things that have no material basis that appear to be vividly real, and they say that daytime appearances are the same. For this school, genuine reality is consciousness, free from the mistaken duality of perceiving subjects and perceived objects. This school is sometimes referred to as the Yogachara, or "yoga practice," school.

The Madhyamaka, or "Middle Way," school includes two schools: the *Rangtong*, or "Self-Empty Middle Way," and the *Shentong*, or "Empty-of-Other Middle Way." Rangtong is further divided into the *Svatantrika*, or Autonomy, subschool, and the *Prasangika*, or Consequence, subschool. Therefore the next stage of investigation is named after the first of these, the Svatantrika subschool. This school says that conventionally things appear to be real, but when investigated with reasoning, nothing can be found to exist. Genuine reality is empty like space.

The next stage is named after the Prasangika subschool. This school describes apparent reality the way ordinary people describe it: without any analysis at all. They say that genuine reality is free from all concepts of what it might be, even the concept of emptiness itself.

The last stage is named after the Shentong Madhyamaka school, which describes apparent reality the same way as the Chittamatra school, while describing genuine reality as luminous clarity, or the inseparability of emptiness and wisdom.

There is one thing to bear in mind about these maps of the path. It is only from the point of view of our confusion that there is a journey to be made at all. From the perspective of genuine reality, there is no journey, no one to make the journey, and no goal to arrive at. Everything is originally pure, great perfection. However, until we realize this, we definitely need to make efforts on the path, because the illusory appearances of the path will unerringly give rise to the illusory appearances of fruition.

3

STARTING TO CONTEMPLATE

THERE ARE MANY TRADITIONS of contemplation, also referred to as "reflection," "investigation," and "analytical meditation." I will make some suggestions based on what I do. You
should experiment to develop ways of contemplating that work
best for you.

Posture is important. I like to contemplate in the place where
I meditate, cross-legged, on a cushion on the floor, with a small
table in front of me to place a text. Sometimes I sit on a chair at
my desk. Wherever you sit, have a relaxed, upright posture. Keep
your back straight—but not rigid—and have a good sense of your
head and shoulders. As is said:

> When your body is straight, the channels are straight;
> When the channels are straight, the energies are straight;
> When the energies are straight, the mind is straight.[1]

When you slump over, you will become dreamy and wander. If
you are too rigid, your mind will become scattered or agitated.

Contemplation is not the same as reading. When you read,
you can cover a lot of ground without really bringing your doubts
and uncertainties to the surface. You can go along with what is
written, giving it "the benefit of the doubt," even when you don't

really see it that way. When you finish reading, you might find that some of the points stick with you, but the more challenging elements may have slipped away.

When you are trying to understand the view, you need to set aside time to really chew on the material, particularly when it goes against your habitual way of thinking. Contemplating half a page is usually enough for one session. It may not seem like it at first, but a page of profound material is a lot to take in. Choose a short selection of text or a few verses to work with, such as the ones in this book. You can also work with long texts by reading them through but stopping to contemplate sections that are pithy or difficult.

It is important to alternate between investigating and analyzing, and then letting go of the investigation and analysis to just rest. If you don't, you might cover over prajna with discursiveness rather than allow it to arise naturally. Take your time. Don't rush.

I start a session by letting my mind settle. When I feel ready, I read a first verse or paragraph a couple of times. Sometimes I need to go back over a line or a few words several times until the meaning is clear. Then I rest again. After a bit, I reread the verse or paragraph. Then I move on to the next part of the selection.

Here is a guided contemplation, using the verse from Dharmakirti quoted in the first chapter, for you to experiment with:

- Begin the session by briefly recollecting your teachers and the Three Jewels, and make the wish to develop realization for the benefit of limitless beings, which is the bodhichitta aspiration.
- Let your mind rest for a few minutes. You can use a meditation technique if you like, but you don't have to.
- Next, read the following verse to yourself:

When there is self, one believes there is other,
From these images of self and other come attach-
     ment and aversion,
As a result of getting wrapped up in these,
All possible faults arise.

- Make sure you understand the meaning of the words. You might need to read the verse several times to see how it fits together. Even a short verse like this has a lot of elements and interconnections, not all of which will be obvious at first. Sometimes you might feel a little panic that you can't understand what's being contemplated. That is okay. Rest with that panic.
- Start with whatever jumps out at you. This helps cut through any anxiety you might feel about doing it right. You could ask yourself basic questions like, "What does this really mean?" or "How does this relate to my experience?" It's like stepping back and saying, "OK, what the heck is going on here?" This could lead to asking, "What is self?" for example.
- After a couple of minutes, read the verse again. Ask yourself further questions, such as "What does 'when there is self' mean? When is there no self?" or "How does 'other' come from calling something 'self'?" Sometimes it helps to try to visualize what is being described.
- Rest with the meaning for a few more minutes.
- Finish the session by letting your mind rest again, and then dedicate the merit of the practice to enlightenment for the benefit of all beings.

One important point is that it helps to not be too sophisticated about the questioning process. Simpler is better. Imagine what it feels like for a young child to try to fit Lego blocks together or work with Play-Doh. That is the way to go about it.

If you get a glimmer of the profound meaning of the quotation, that's great, but don't try to hold on to it. We all need to investigate again and again in order to overcome our deep habituation to believing the self is real. If you don't get a glimmer, don't worry. Ask yourself some more basic questions, such as "What is this 'I'?" or "Who is contemplating this verse?" Then let it go. Finding good questions is much more important than finding answers.

You could do a contemplation like this in fifteen or twenty minutes.

GROUP CONTEMPLATION PRACTICE

Contemplation is also an excellent group practice. It doesn't take much to bring out people's intelligence. One person's spark usually stimulates other people's insights. I have done a lot of group contemplation, and with pithy material it is a lot of fun. Ponlop Rinpoche's Nitartha Institute developed a very nice format for group contemplation:

- A teacher or senior student leads the session.
- First, everyone reads a section out loud together and contemplates.
- After a few minutes, the leader reads the section again to the group.
- After another few minutes, everyone reads the section together again out loud.
- Depending on the material, after one, two, or sometimes three sections are contemplated, people discuss their understanding and experience of the contemplation.

A key element is that during the discussion, emphasis should be placed on people's present experience, not what they studied or experienced sometime in the past. This keeps the discussion from getting discursive and will focus it and make it experiential.

In a longer session, you might go on to do more contemplations after the first discussion, but don't try to do too much. People will lose their focus and might start to get irritable. If you are doing a ninety-minute session, then thirty to forty-five minutes of contemplation, interspersed with discussions, is reasonable.

Group contemplation is a good alternative to discussion groups at dharma programs. Leading a group contemplation is also a good way for people to begin to teach material that they have not yet mastered. Many people who normally don't like discussion groups find this format refreshing and enjoyable.

4

SELFLESSNESS 101

LET'S TAKE A CLOSER look at what "I" and "me" are all about. First, we will look at the way the self appears. Then, we can begin to see the way it actually is.

Consider the fact that sometimes we say, "I am sick," and at other times we say, "I have a headache." In the first case, it seems that the "I" itself is ill. In the second, "I" and the pain seem to be two different things, with the self possessing the pain of the headache. Sometimes we even say, "I was not myself the other day," as if "I" and "the self" are two separate things. The first thing to note is that while it seems completely obvious that there is such a thing as the self, when we try to pin down what the self is, the whole thing becomes completely elusive.

Once the great yogi Milarepa met a young shepherd boy who wanted to learn about Milarepa's teachings and asked him if people had one mind or many (which is like asking if there is one self or many selves). Milarepa told him to look at his own mind and find out. The next day the shepherd reported:

"Lama-la, yesterday evening I asked you how many minds there are. I have looked and seen that there is no more than one. As for this one mind, though, you can try to kill it but you can't kill it; you can try to chase after it and grab it but you can't catch it, and you cannot push it down either. If you put it somewhere, it doesn't stay; if you send it some-where, it doesn't go; if you try to gather it in, it doesn't come; if you look at it, you can't see it; if you investigate, you can't find it; if you think it exists, it doesn't show itself, and if you think it doesn't exist, it flows out everywhere. It flickers here and there; it darts to and fro; it hops around bippity bop boop beep de beep bop bop de boop bop beep de boom!*And sometimes it just spaces out and you don't know what happened. I have no idea what mind is."[1]

What can we say about the elusive "I" and "me"? These words must refer to something—but what? Maybe we can't describe the self precisely, but most of us would agree that it seems to have four characteristics: it appears to be *one thing*; it appears to be *independent*; it appears to be *lasting*; and it appears to be *important*.

The first characteristic, that the self appears to be one thing, is often called *singularity*, meaning that we feel the self to be a single thing. Except perhaps when we experience extreme psychological states, we don't think that we have multiple selves that we cycle through or choose from. We don't get up in the morning and think, "Today I will be Jane, and perhaps tonight I will try out being Judy." We think we are the same person all the time. We might have different personalities in different sit-uations, but this is like the self putting on different clothing, not changing selves. This is what the shepherd reported to Milarepa.

The second characteristic is *independence*. We think the self makes choices; for example, we can decide to do the dishes, or

---

* The translator, Ari Goldfield, notes this translates the Tibetan experien-tial terms *rig rig*, *tur tur*, and *treh treh*, which have the meaning of rapid movement in the sense of flickering, darting, and hopping. Since they are impossible to translate literally, an attempt was made to find an English equivalent.

watch television, or go out to dinner and a movie. We don't think that what we do simply emerges from the ether due to causes and conditions over which we have no control.

The third characteristic, that the self appears to be lasting, is referred to as *permanence* because the Buddhist teachings generally define permanence as anything that lasts a second moment. The self appears to be lasting or permanent because it feels like we have had the same self all our lives. While our bodily appearance changes, and our knowledge and experiences change, the self doesn't seem to change. I vividly remember my father-in-law saying on his eighty-third birthday that he didn't feel that he was any different from when he was a child. He didn't really feel older. It was a very interesting comment and clearly illustrates this third characteristic.

The fourth characteristic is *importance*. Like the other characteristics, we might take this one for granted. Even if we don't go around thinking, "I need to look out for number one," self-importance is the undercurrent to all our activity. We only have to recall what we are like when we are stuck in traffic or cooling our heels in the doctor's waiting room to see how important we feel we are. Few of us think, "I don't need to get to work any more than the rest of the people stuck in this traffic jam." In fact, we are usually so absorbed in our own agenda that we can't even imagine anyone else having anything important to do.

THE ENEMY INSIDE

Here are two contemplations that you can work with to bring out what the self is like. The first contemplation is from Nawang Gehlek Rimpoche's recent book, *Good Life, Good Death:*

> The true enemy is inside. The maker of trouble, the source of all our suffering, the destroyer of our joy, and the

destroyer of our virtue is inside. It is Ego. I call it, "I, the most precious one."

"I, the most precious one" does not serve any purpose. It only makes tremendous, unreasonable, impossible demands. Ego wants to be the best and has no consideration for anyone else. Things work fine as long as "I, the most precious one's" wishes are being fulfilled. But when they're not, and Ego turns on the self, it becomes self-hatred. That self-hatred will eventually burn the house down.

First, Ego separates me from the rest of the world and sees "I" and "me" as the most important. Then "I" becomes "my," as in my friend, my enemy. I love my friend. I hate my enemy. I help my friend. I harm my enemy. That's where attachment and hatred begin. They don't come out of the blue.

Then the concept of "my" gathers strength. "My" becomes important to me. An ordinary cup, when it becomes my cup, is worth more. So, too, are my body, my country, my religion, or my sect.[2]

The second contemplation is from the chapter on "Patience" in Shantideva's eighth-century classic *The Way of the Bodhisattva*:

This self, if permanent,
Is certainly impassible like space itself.
And should it meet with other factors,
How should they affect it, since it is unchanging?

If, when things occur, it stays unchanged and as before,
What influence has action had on it?
They say that this affects the Self,
But what connection could there be between them?[3]

Singular, independent, lasting, and important: this is how we define the self. And as Gehlek Rimpoche adds, it "does not serve any purpose" except as "the source of all our suffering."

In addition to the four characteristics of the self, we can also talk about two basic aspects of this troublemaker. The first aspect—the *imputed self*—is the identity we attribute to the self based on all the relational, philosophical, and religious concepts we have about who and what we are. "I am . . ." a nurse, a geek, a human, a musician, a father, a child, a good writer, an idiot, the boss, a bodhisattva, a child of God—whatever. The Judeo-Christian notion of a soul, or the Hindu notion of atman are also examples of the imputed self. The second aspect is the *instinctive self*. This refers to the grunt level of feeling "I exist!" before there are any words to express that. These are the two main ways the self appears.

Now we can begin to investigate what the self really is. One way to pin down this vague and elusive appearance is to ask some simple questions; for example, "Is the self the body or is it the mind? Is it both of these, or is it neither of them?"

Most of us would say that the self is both the body and the mind. Yet, the body is something tangible and substantial. It seems to be made of physical matter, however we would like to describe that—for example, as cells, as molecules, as atoms, as subatomic particles, and so on. The mind, on the other hand, seems to be immaterial. It is not made of particles. Even though scientists can now correlate mental activity with changing electrical activity in the brain, no one proposes that thoughts, emotions, consciousness, and the other mental phenomena are material substances.

How could the self be both material and immaterial? We are not discussing some machine with different components, some of which are made out of metal and some of which are made out of plastic. We are asking how one thing—the self—could be made up of two things that have *no common basis*? How could that possibly work? How could they be connected? If something is not made of any matter, what could possibly attach to it? What could hold it together? As Mr. Spock would say, "That is not logical."

If we accept that the self cannot be both the body and the mind, we need to explore the possibility that it is just one or the other of these. What if the self is just the mind? That leads to the absurd conclusion that an immaterial mind could possess a material body. How could something immaterial possess something material? Again we have to ask, how could they be connected? A further problem with this idea is that if the self is just the mind, how would you know when you stubbed your toe? The body would be something separate from the self, like a piece of furniture.

Next, we need to ask whether the self could just be the body. This leads to the absurd conclusion that a material body could possess or connect with an immaterial mind. Also, if the self is just the body, how could you know anything, since it is mind that knows? If the self is just the body, it follows that a corpse would be a self! Mr. Spock?

By the way, at the time of the Buddha, some Indian philosophers said that mind arose from the elements. Around the same time, Greek materialists held similar views. Many contemporary western scientists seem to have similar beliefs. These scientists say that mind is just "an emergent property" of the brain. Emergent properties are said to be phenomena seen in complex systems that are not properties of any of the parts of the system, and not produced by merely adding the parts together.

Nobel laureate Francis Crick, codiscoverer of the double helix structure of DNA, wrote, "You, your joys and your sorrows, your memories and your ambitions, your sense of personal identity and free will, are in fact no more than the behavior of a vast assembly of nerve cells and their associated molecules."[4] In other words, he asserts that the subjective sense of "you," meaning mind or consciousness, is just an emergent property of matter.

However, this view does not give an answer to the question of how immaterial mind could arise from a material brain. The brain is visibly observable. It has shape, color, and mass. It can be touched. Mind has none of these visible or tactile properties, but it is that which knows. How could the entity of mind arise from the entity of the body, with which it shares no common properties?

There is one more possibility that we need to look at. If the self cannot be both the body and the mind, or just the mind, or just the body, can it be something that is neither the body nor the mind? If such a self really exists, it should be observable in some way. Can you find such a self? How could such a self possess both a material body and an immaterial mind?

At this point, you might start to dismiss this whole investigation as a silly word game that is both irritating and ridiculous. However, before you do, consider the possibility that vagueness and elusiveness form ego's outer layer and that ego uses irritation and indignation to fortify itself when any attempt is made to look into what the self actually is. These reactions help maintain the illusion of the self, even when the unreasonableness of that illusion is clearly pointed out.

You might wonder how such intangible qualities as vagueness, elusiveness, and irritation could perform such powerful functions, but that is the secret of ego's whole system. The self is not made of any substance at all: it is just a kaleidoscopic display of empty imagery, intangible, like a self in a dream. As Chögyam Trungpa explains in *Transcending Madness*:

> These experiences . . . are space, different versions of space. It seems intense and solid, but in actual fact it isn't at all. They are different aspects of space—that's the exciting or interesting part. In fact, it is complete open space, without any colors or any particularly solid way of relating.[5]

Here is another contemplation that might help clarify this. It is probably the shortest text you will ever contemplate, but I have found it to be one of the most potent. I come back to it again and again. It is one of "the four mistaken conceptions":*

"We have taken what is not a self to be a self."

To do this contemplation you need to take a close look at what "me" feels like and ask, "What do I take to be a self? What is that like? Is there anything there other than just some vague changing sensations?"

We can come at this investigation of the self from a different angle by looking at René Descartes's famous conclusion to his own investigation of the self: "I think, therefore I am." There is a traditional Buddhist image that is relevant here. Imagine walking into a pottery studio and seeing a spinning potter's wheel with a half-finished vase turning around on top. Looking at this scene, you would instinctively feel that there must be a potter nearby. This is also what happens when we observe our thoughts and imagine that there must be a thinker. Yet whenever we look, we can't find any thinker. We never see thoughts *and* something producing thought. We just see more thoughts.

You could ask yourself, "What is this thinker like?" If the answer is that it is the self, then you might be going around in circles like the potter's wheel! Can you perceive the thinker? Is it one of those animated machines inside your head like the ones they show in pain-relief commercials? Is there a little man or woman in there? Is it the brain? If you think it is the brain, try to imagine how a mass of gray matter can produce the thoughts you experience. Where do they come out?

---

* The other three are, "We have taken what is not clean to be clean, we have taken what is impermanent to be permanent, and we have taken what is suffering to be pleasure."

To conclude this chapter, here is one more verse for you to contemplate. This is from Chandrakirti, the seventh-century author of one of the most profound Buddhist texts, one that is still intensively studied, called the *Madhyamakavatara,* or *Entering the Middle Way.* This is a good verse to contemplate because it both presents the essence of ego clinging and expresses the aspiration to help all beings who are suffering from this delusion:

> First, thinking "me," they cling to self,
> Then, thinking "this is mine," attachment to things
>   develops.
> Beings are powerless, like buckets rambling in a well—
> I bow to compassion for these wanderers.[6]

5

VAIBHASHIKA
Taking Things Apart

EACH SCHOOL'S METHODS have unique and profound insights to offer. This is easy to overlook when the emphasis is on the way "higher" systems correct flaws in "lower" systems, particularly since we naturally want to identify with the highest views of all. Here, we will look at the methods in terms of their increasing subtlety rather than their dialectical progression. As we journey along this path, try to see how each school's insights unlock your understanding in unpredictable and complementary ways. Approaching the view from many angles will deepen your understanding and gradually lead to profound experience.

We begin with the first level, the Vaibhashika. Vaibhashikas love to take things apart. I was probably a Vaibhashika in a previous life, because when I was a child I loved to take things apart. My mother was constantly telling me things like, "Put down the peppermill. You will make a mess!" and "Don't take apart my alarm clock! You'll wreck it." On the other hand, when I managed to put them back together or repair things, she called me "Handy Andy."

What do Vaibhashika methods take apart? They take apart things held together by concepts. Here is the way Vasubandhu presents the system of the Vaibhashikas in *The Treasury of Abhi-dharma* (*Abhidharmakosha*):

> If something is physically destroyed or mentally broken
> down,
> The mental state that apprehended it does not engage
> it any more.
> Something like a vase or water exists seemingly,
> While what exists genuinely is something other.[1]

What this means is that we usually see things in a coarse way that covers over a tremendous variety and diversity of appearances and prevents us from recognizing genuine reality. This school's method is to look closely and precisely at experience to cut through our habitual way of seeing.

Imagine for a moment that you are working in a laboratory where you prepare tissue samples for viewing under a microscope. To do this, you use a special slicer to cut extremely thin sections of tissue so that the microscope's light can pass through to produce an image. This is how Vaibhashikas work with experience. They look at it precisely, microscopically, by slicing it into the subtlest possible moments.

IMPERMANENCE AND MORE IMPERMANENCE

One way to do this is by looking at subtle impermanence. Buddhists talk about two types of impermanence. Both are extremely important. The gross form of impermanence is called "the impermanence of the continuum." This describes the way everything that appears to exist—people, houses, trees, automobiles—ages and disintegrates. This is called the impermanence of the continuum because the things that are aging seem to form a continuous series of instances that blend into each other. Think of the way a child looks when it is born, then when it is three months old, then a year old, three years old, five years old. Understanding this type of impermanence, and taking it to heart, is important because if we understand that all things age and disintegrate, then we will understand that we, too, must age and disintegrate. No matter what the television commercials and glossy magazine ads promise, since we are going to age and disintegrate, we had better do more than apply expensive face cream if we want to deal with the disintegration to come.

The other form of impermanence is "subtle impermanence." This describes the fact that all phenomena change from moment to moment. When we get out our microscope, we see that nothing lasts a second moment. All is change. As the Buddha said in the *Diamond Cutter Sutra*, all phenomena are "Like a star at dawn, like a bubble in a mountain stream, like a flash of lightning in a summer cloud, like a flickering lamp, a phantom, and a dream."

A candle flame (a type of flickering lamp) is a good example of subtle momentary impermanence. What happens when we go into a restaurant or a shrine room and see candles burning? If we see a candle flame, look away, and later notice the flame again, we think that it is the same candle flame that we saw burning a few minutes before. In fact, it is not. The first instance of the candle flame is completely gone. Because the two images look so similar, we take them to be one thing. We make this mistake all the time when we see objects, faces, houses, rivers, or landscapes. We do not recognize subtle impermanence. Thought covers it over. This is a good example of something that " . . . exists seemingly, while what exists genuinely is something other." (The candle itself is a good example of the impermanence of the continuum: the many instants of the candle seem to form one continuum that gets shorter and shorter as the candle burns away.)

Here is another example. Think about the many different moments of experience that we take to be the body. The experience of bathing can be used to illustrate this. I usually shower and shave in the morning. Substitute your own bathing habits as we go along.

When I shower, I close my eyes to keep the water out. Looking microscopically at the details of my experience in the shower, there are many tactile sensations: hand on soap, hands washing feet, hot water on back, rubbing hands on face, hands on tiles, hands washing shoulder, and so on. When I finish washing and turn off the water, I open my eyes, and the details shift to visible forms: seeing a forearm, hand wiping off excess water, seeing tiles, hand picking up towel, drying torso. When I get out of the shower and stand in front of the mirror, the visible forms become reflection of face, reflection of chest, and so forth. Each one of these lasts only a moment, and then it is gone. When it is gone, it is completely gone. I can find similar experiences, but each of the moments of experience is unique.

When we don't look closely at the details of these sights and sensations, we take them all to be "my body" or "I am taking a shower." Thought obscures, or covers over, the details of our sensory experience. When we put experience under the microscope, we see a series of dramatically different moments. We think that the body must be in there somewhere, but when we look closely, we don't find anything that is "my body," just the constantly changing series of experiences. Body is a concept superimposed on these moments. Thought conceals experience—that is what this investigation points to. According to Vaibhashikas, each of these moments is genuinely real. The collection of these moments is just a concept that is imputed by thought. Taking apart our experience like this helps separate our ideas about the way things appear from what is genuinely real.

DECONSTRUCTING THOUGHTS

We can apply the same type of investigation to the continuum of the mind. We think the mind is one thing, one stream of consciousness that is unbroken from the time we were born until now, but when we look for such a continuum, we can't find it. When we look at each of the experiences that make up that continuum, the same thing happens. If we look at a thought, for instance, that thought seems to be one thing, but you can divide the thought into a part that is past, a part that is present, and a part that is yet to come. Each of these parts can also be divided into smaller parts.

Take the thought "I would like to have lunch." At the moment you think "I," the part "would like to have lunch," has not yet arisen. When you think "like to have," the part "I would," is already gone, and "lunch," has not yet arisen. When you think "lunch," the part "I would like to have," is already gone. Like this, we can see that thoughts are also made up of lots of moments. The whole thought is just a concept that is superimposed on all these moments. Surprisingly, it is very hard to see our thoughts because they are obscured by thought!

When we investigate our body and mind in this way, we find lots of different moments of experience, but we don't find anything that is "body" or "mind." Again, while these things seem to exist, "What exists genuinely is something other." Here are two quotations that will help you contemplate this. Both are from Chögyam Trungpa. The first one is from *The Heart of the Buddha*:

> We think we are great, broadly significant, and that we cover a whole large area. We see ourselves as having a history and a future, and here we are in our big-deal present. But if we look at ourselves clearly in this very moment, we see we are just grains of sand — just little people concerned only with this little dot which is called nowness.[2]

The second contemplation is from *Cutting Through Spiritual Materialism*:

According to the Buddhist tradition, the spiritual path is the process of cutting through our confusion, of uncovering the awakened state of mind. . . . The heart of the confusion is that man has a sense of self which seems to him to be continuous and solid. When a thought or emotion or event occurs, there is a sense of someone being conscious of what is happening. You sense that *you* are reading these words. This sense of self is actually a transitory, discontinuous event, which in our confusion seems to be quite solid and continuous. Since we take our confused view as being real, we struggle to maintain and enhance this solid self.[3]

Having looked microscopically at experience, Vaibhashikas investigate further for the basis of this "sense of self" through a process of sorting or triage. If you had a huge pile of change that you thought might contain a precious gold coin, you could thoroughly search through the pile using a coin sorter like the ones you find in banks. You would scoop coins into the machine and it would sort them into whatever denominations your coins come in: pennies, nickels, dimes, quarters, and so on. If there was a gold coin there, it would be easy to find. This is the way Vaibhashikas search for the self. They set up a series of categories that cover the entire range of phenomena and use it as a framework to sort through their experience to see if they can find a self.

THE FIVE SKANDHAS

One set of categories used for this investigation is known as "the five skandhas." *Skandha* is a Sanskrit word that means "heap, aggregate, or collection." The collection of the five skandhas is referred to by such evocative terms as "disintegrating collections" or the "transitory collections," which convey the sense of the dynamic, constantly changing content of the skandhas.

The names of the five skandhas are:

1. The skandha of forms
2. The skandha of feelings (or sensations)
3. The skandha of discriminations (or perceptions)
4. The skandha of formations
5. The skandha of consciousnesses

Mipham Gyamtso Rinpoche says in *The Gateway to Knowledge*, "All phenomena which are conditioned things are included within these five aggregates. They are the basis from which many systems come about."[4] In other words, the aggregates, or skandhas, include everything that we could ever experience.

The *skandha of forms* includes the five sense faculties and their objects. The sense faculties are the eye, the ear, the nose, the tongue, and the body. Their objects consist of visible forms for the eye, sounds for the ear, smells for the nose, tastes for the tongue, and tactile sensations for the body. This first skandha includes all that we usually think of as the outer and inner material world, but viewed microscopically, not conceptualized as coarse things.

The *skandha of feelings* consists of all the pleasant, unpleasant, and indifferent sensations that we experience; in other words, our most basic reactions for and against things.

The *skandha of discriminations* includes all clinging to characteristics, qualities, or distinguishing features. This includes everything from clinging to such characteristics as the color and shape of visible objects up to clinging to the pleasant qualities of our friends and the unpleasant qualities of our enemies.

The *skandha of formations* includes all thoughts, emotions, and mental states that are not included in the other four skandhas. Formations are what make mind move toward various objects. They are the thoroughly created mental states. They consist of thoughts including names, words, letters, and other concepts; emotions; and mental states. Mental states can be virtuous, nonvirtuous, or neutral. The virtuous states include such things as faith, conscientiousness, equanimity, nonattachment, nonaggression, and diligence. The nonvirtuous states include such things as ignorance, attachment, anger, arrogance, doubt, resentment, hostility, pretentiousness, and self-infatuation. There are also neutral states that can become either virtuous or nonvirtuous states, such as regret and analysis.

Sometimes there are said to be forty-nine mental states and sometimes fifty or fifty-one, but as Mipham Rinpoche says, "It should be understood, however, that there are a tremendous number of different kinds, such as sadness and elation, difficulty and ease, patience and impatience, and so forth, which result from the different kinds of grasping patterns of apprehension, perception and so on."[5]

Consciousness is defined as "that which is aware of objects." It is the clear, knowing aspect of each experience. If you deliberately move your awareness to different parts of your body such as your fingers, ears, toes, and so on, you will easily understand the meaning of the term. The *skandha of consciousnesses* consists of what are called the six primary consciousnesses: the eye sense consciousness, the ear sense consciousness, the nose sense consciousness, the tongue sense consciousness, the body sense consciousness, and the mind or mental consciousness. This is the general Buddhist presentation.

Some schools include two additional consciousnesses in their presentations. The seventh consciousness is the *klesha* consciousness, or disturbed mental consciousness, which is responsible for maintaining the ongoing basic feeling of duality. The eighth consciousness—called variously the *alaya*, "the all-ground," or "the all-basis consciousness"—is the basic storehouse of experiences.

The skandhas can be presented in much more detail, but this should give you a good idea of how the system works. A good way to visualize the skandhas is to imagine that they are like a fireworks display. Some burst across the mind's sky like gigantic starbursts. Some are more like colorful rockets, zinging into space. Some are like images made of light. Some are like clouds of smoke. The consciousnesses are like our shifting awareness of different parts of the display. The basic point is that they are not solid things but a continuously disintegrating, groundless display.

SORTING FOR A SELF

Using the framework of the skandhas, we can begin to sort through our experience, looking for the basis for the sense of self. When we do, the first thing that becomes obvious is just how shifty experience is. We discussed this in the previous chapter, but using the skandhas to sort through our experience helps show the elusiveness more clearly. For example, ask yourself, "Do the skandhas operate simultaneously or sequentially?" It is very hard to answer this question because experiences change so rapidly. There does seem to be a dominant skandha in each moment, but it is hard to tell if the other skandhas are operating as well.

Does a lot of your experience fall within the skandha of forms? Because the outer and inner material worlds seem so stable and continuous, you would think that the skandha of forms would be a big part of experience. Is that the case? What about the skandha of formations? Generally, I experience flashes of sensory experience punctuating much longer periods of thinking and feeling. Is that true for you?

The mental events of the second, third, and fourth skandhas are incredibly shifty. For example, it seems that we think about one subject for a long time, but when we look closely, each moment is a constantly changing constellation around a central theme, until the theme shifts and a new constellation arises. Do you find anything stable there?

The skandha of consciousnesses seems to take in all of this in a stable way, but that stability is also deceptive. Is there any single consciousness that is separate from the consciousness of a particular object?

This is a key point. You can't find "a consciousness" no matter how hard you look. You always find consciousness of something—a form, a feeling, a perception, or a formation. In fact, since the definition of *consciousness* is "that which is aware of objects"—when there is no object, there is no consciousness. When the object ceases, the consciousness disappears. Even though we often identify consciousness with the sense of self, since we can't find an ongoing consciousness, it can't be the basis for a continuous self.

The more we look, the clearer it is that our experience is composed entirely of these constantly disintegrating collections. We don't find any possessor of the collections. There is nothing that we can point to that corresponds to "me," the self, as we believe we are—one thing, independent, lasting, and important. Because of this constant shiftiness and lack of a solid landing place, we experience a very subtle and pervasive sense of agitation, restlessness, or dissatisfaction that is woven into the basic fabric of our experience. It is this restlessness that keeps mind moving and the display of the skandhas proliferating. This is what is known as "all-pervasive suffering," or the suffering of conditioned existence.

A Logical Analysis

The protector Nagarjuna examines the relationship of the self to the aggregates in *The Fundamental Wisdom of the Middle Way*. The following verse from that text makes a very good basis for contemplation:

> If the self were the aggregates,
> It would be something that arises and ceases.
> If the self were something other than the aggregates,
> It would not have the aggregates' characteristics.[6]

If the self were the same thing as the aggregates, the self would constantly be rising and ceasing, because forms, feelings, discriminations, formations, and consciousnesses are constantly arising and ceasing, as we have seen. Since the self seems to be continuous, the aggregates can't be the self. Also, if the self were the same as the aggregates, there would be many selves, just as there are many aggregates. Since the self seems to be one thing, the aggregates can't be the self. The aggregates also can't be the self, because if they were, the self could not "have" a body, feelings, discriminations, thoughts, emotions, mental states, and consciousnesses. It doesn't make sense to say something possesses itself.

On the other hand, if the self were a completely different thing from the aggregates, we should be able to observe such a self directly, but we don't. Also, such a self would have no characteristics and be beyond experience, since "All phenomena which are conditioned things are included within these five aggregates."

This is an important method for determining selflessness, and I encourage you to contemplate Nagarjuna's verse again and again.

Finally, Khenchen Kunzang Palden gives instructions for transforming our first hesitant glimpses of selflessness into real conviction, and eventually experiencing selflessness directly. This quotation comes from his commentary on Shantideva's *The Way of the Bodhisattva*, called *The Nectar of Manjushri's Speech*, which is quoted in *Wisdom: Two Buddhist Commentaries*:

In just this way, if this hesitant questioning is supplanted by a firm conviction that 'the self which is grasped at as the personal identity of the aggregates is nothing but a mere imputation,' and if one becomes accustomed to this, the absence of self will be directly experienced. To this end, it is said in the teachings that one should ask oneself where this sense of 'I' arises, where it is located and abides, and where it subsides. In accordance with this instruction, after making a thorough investigation, one should simply rest in the state of finding nothing. When one is unable to continue with this, one should proceed with the former analytical meditation. These two types of meditation should be practiced alternately.[7]

6

SAUTRANTIKA

What Really Comes to Mind?

WHILE THE VAIBHASHIKA method emphasizes the distinctness of each moment of experience and exhaustively sorts through these experiences searching for a self, the Sautrantika method explores the subtleties of these moments further and points out two very different types of experience: moments of *perception* and moments of *conception*.

Perception is experiencing outer and inner phenomena directly—the eye seeing forms or the ear hearing sounds, for example. Conception is experiencing phenomena indirectly using words and concepts—thinking, "This is a book," for example. The distinction seems obvious, but usually we mix perception and conception and don't know exactly what we are experiencing. When we look closely at the processes of perception and conception, we see that things are not at all what they seem. We notice that we don't clearly experience what appears to our minds. We think we experience things clearly, but generally what we experience are our own projections.

Here is a simple example. Think about the book you are looking at. "Book" is a concept. Your eyes see visible forms, not concepts, yet we think we are looking at something that actually is a book. We blend the visible form with the concept, and think that there is an object in our hands that *really is a book*.

Here is another. Take a moment to look in the mirror. While you are looking, ask yourself whether you are *seeing a reflection* or *seeing your face*. At first the distinction may not be obvious. Keep looking and ask again. If you think you see your face, how did it get inside the mirror?

These two examples point out how we confuse visual experience with concepts about what we are experiencing. The same thing happens with sounds. When you hear something, is it an "automobile" you hear, for example, or is it a *sound*? We *hear* sounds, but we *conceive* of automobiles. We have the same confusions about smells, tastes, and bodily sensations. In each case we superimpose concepts onto sensory experience.

This process of superimposition is lightning-fast, and very subtle. You see someone at a distance, and in an instant you "recognize" them. What this really means is that you project a concept of that person and then label it. When a friend shaves off a mustache he has had for many years, you might not notice the difference because you "know who he is," with or without the mustache, almost before you look at him!

Similar confusions take place when we think about things. Take, for example, sitting at home thinking about being back in high school, listening to our favorite teacher. We mix our concepts of the teacher and the school with the actual experience of being in that place, and wind up thinking they are the same thing. After a moment, we don't know where we are. Are we sitting in a chair at home or sitting at a desk in high school? This is another way we confuse concepts with direct experience. We don't see the way conceptual mind actually functions.

Blending together conceptions and perceptions prevents us from seeing either clearly. We don't really know what we are experiencing. We can't get rid of concepts—and in fact we don't need to get rid of concepts. We need to be able to see concepts clearly for what they are, and see sense perceptions clearly for what they are. When we blend concepts and sense perceptions together, we experience what are referred to as "coarse" objects. We need to deconstruct these objects so that our projections no longer lead us around by the nose (which is the basic dynamic of samsara).

Ponlop Rinpoche explains this as follows:

> We are confused by the appearing thing—the conceptual mind takes [what appears to] it to be an outer object. The conceptual mind cannot distinguish between the image of an object that appears to it and the real (external) object. It takes them to be one.[1]

This is worth reflecting on.

VALID COGNITION

To clarify these confusions, Sautrantikas use a sophisticated system of analysis drawn from a tradition known as *pramana*,* or "valid cognition," in order to look closely at perception and conception. The valid-cognition tradition uses a precise framework to describe the way these processes work. Pramana is a complex topic in many ways, but its basic insights provide powerful ways of exploring our experience.

Before we look at this framework, we need to know a few technical terms. Many of us freeze up when we are introduced to technical terms. If you have ever tried to explain computer software to someone, or if you have had to have software explained to you, you know what I mean. (In the unlikely event you've been lucky enough to miss these experiences, you probably know what

---

* This is the tradition of Dignaga and Dharmakirti, who gathered together and systematized the various teachings of the Buddha on the nature of knowledge, in the sixth and seventh centuries.

I mean if you've ever tried to read an insurance policy or other document sprinkled with technical terms.) Hopefully, this won't be so traumatic. If you find that the terms make you go blank, relax and loosen up. Try to remember, these concepts are about ordinary, kitchen-sink experience—you *can* understand them.

The key to unlocking the power of the Sautrantika method comes from understanding the meaning of a pair of awkward terms: *specifically characterized phenomena* and *generally characterized phenomena*.

Let's start with specifically characterized phenomena. Specifically characterized phenomena are the objects of direct perception. They appear to nonconceptual consciousnesses. They appear clearly, in a detailed way. When you look at an azalea or an iris, the object, the flower itself, appears clearly, in great detail. That object of your eye consciousness is a specifically characterized phenomenon.

The taste of candy on your tongue is another example that the Sutra school uses to illustrate specifically characterized phenomena. No concept can really describe what this taste is like. We can try to label it, but the labels are arbitrary. They can't convey the actual taste to someone who has not eaten that type of candy. Yet, the actual experience is vivid, clear, and unique. This taste is a specifically characterized phenomenon.

Generally characterized phenomena appear to conceptual consciousnesses, or conceptual mind. They appear as vague images, in a cloudy way. When you think of flowers in general, a vague image that somehow encompasses all of the flowers you have experienced appears. It is not clear and detailed, *but it does appear*. This image is a generally characterized phenomenon.

You might wonder about the images of particular things that appear to your mind, such as remembering your mother or father or the home you grew up in. These seem more detailed than the concepts "parents" and "houses," but they are still general images, because they encompass all of your experience of your parents and childhood home. This type of generally character-ized phenomenon is called an *object generality*.*

To summarize: perception experiences specifically character-ized phenomena, and conception experiences generally charac-terized phenomena. These are the two types of phenomena that appear to our minds. In this tradition these two are called *appear-ing objects*.

Here is a quotation from Khenpo Tsültrim that points out the way conceptuality is confused about appearances. Since it is rather long for a contemplation, it would be good to contemplate it slowly and carefully.

What is the meaning of appearance? Generally, there are two kinds of objects: appearing objects and referent objects. What actually appears to a mind [or a conscious-ness] is called an appearing object. All minds have appear-ing objects. All consciousnesses have appearing objects.

Conceptual consciousnesses have referent objects [what the concept refers to]. Nonconceptual conscious-nesses do not have referent objects. For instance, the consciousnesses of the five gates [the five sense conscious-nesses] have appearing objects but do not have referent objects.

The specifically characterized things that are the bases of designation for the names *visible form, sound, smell, taste,* and *tangible object* only appear nakedly; thus, [the consciousnesses that apprehend them] do not have refer-ent objects. . . .

Conceptual consciousnesses have referent objects. They have both appearing objects and referent objects.

* There is some disagreement about this type of experience; some teachers say that what appears is a mixture of specifically characterized and gener-ally characterized phenomena.

The appearance right in the face of a conceptual consciousness is a generally characterized phenomenon. It is not clear: general characteristics appear.

The specifically characterized phenomenon is the referent object. A conceptual consciousness thinks the specifically characterized phenomenon and the generally characterized phenomenon are one. For instance, if you think now about the tall buildings in New York City, an image of those tall buildings appears to your thought. An image of those tall buildings appears to mind. It is a generally characterized phenomenon. The tall buildings that are in New York City—the bases of designation [what the term "the tall buildings that are in New York City" refers to]—are not here. They are in New York. The specifically characterized phenomena that are the bases of designation are the referent object. The conceptual consciousness makes that connection. The image—the likeness of those buildings—is a generally characterized phenomenon. That generally characterized phenomenon is what actually appears to the conceptual consciousness.

The referent object does not appear to the conceptual consciousness at all. We do not see New York's tall buildings now. However, we refer to them. In determining an image of New York's tall buildings, which is what appears to a conceptual consciousness, and the tall buildings themselves, which exist somewhere else, to be one, a conceptual consciousness makes a mistake. A conceptual consciousness has both an appearing object, which is a generally characterized phenomenon, and a referent object, which is a specifically characterized phenomenon. It mistakenly considers the appearing object and the referent object to be one. It engages its objects through mistakenly considering them to be one.[2]

Here is the basic point: we spend a great deal of time thinking about things, but that thinking is mistaken.

What are the implications of this mistake? What it comes down to is that all of the people, places, and things that appear to our conceptual minds are not actual people, places, and things. We can only think about generally characterized phenomena— abstractions. These abstractions may resemble the specifically characterized phenomena that we confuse them with, but even when there is a resemblance, it is always as vague as the resemblance of a description of candy to the actual taste.

When our conceptions resemble the specifically characterized phenomena they refer to, they can be extremely useful. All communication and abstract thinking depends on them. Often, however, our abstractions have little correspondence to the things they refer to. For example, think of all the times you have imagined future situations that you hoped for or feared—what they would be like, what you would say, how you would handle things—and when the situations actually occurred, they had nothing in common with what you imagined.

This type of confusion about appearances permeates all of our experience. To use conceptions effectively and accurately, we need to overcome this confusion. We need to recognize how appearances dawn. This (again) is like recognizing a dream to be a dream while you are dreaming. Here are three investigations you can do to recognize appearances in an unmixed way.

Try not to struggle with the contemplations. It is better to do each one a number of times, for short periods, than to wrestle with them for longer periods. Since we have been mistaking the nature of appearances for as long as we can imagine, our habitual patterns are very thick. You might get glimpses during the investigations, or they might come later on.

Here are some pointers for the investigations:

- Try to notice what arises in your mind.
- Try to see if what you are thinking about has a location in space. Is it right in front of you, or is it off to one side? Does it move about?
- Do you notice only the discursive mind, or is that discursiveness describing something that seems to be before you?
- If you notice both things, try to see which came first, the discursiveness or the generally characterized phenomenon.

First, bring to mind an object of desire: a person or thing you want to possess. It could be someone you would like to get closer to, or a car you would like to own, something else you would like to buy, or some special status you would like to receive. Think about the object a little until your desire becomes vivid. At this point, let go of the discursive thoughts about the object and see if you can locate the object itself. Ask yourself, "Does the object of desire have specific characteristics or only general ones?" and "Is it like seeing the 'actual' object of desire or only an abstract image of that object?"

It is hard to explain how to tease the appearing object and referent object apart. It is something you need to experiment with for yourself. You can try to see if the object that comes to mind is located somewhere in your vicinity, and then imagine where the specifically characterized phenomenon that your object is based on is actually located.

When things we would like to possess come to mind, we usually only notice their positive qualities. One easy way of teasing apart these phenomena is to remember that the actual object of your desire will not be 100 percent pleasing!

Next, think of someone who has hurt your feelings: a colleague, friend, child, or parent. This object will probably become vivid very quickly. Don't let it carry you away. You might need to spend a little time acknowledging painful feelings before going on with the investigation. You don't have to get rid of the pain, just acknowledge it and let it be. Then look to see what the object is like. Again ask yourself, "Does the object that caused me harm have specific characteristics or only general ones?" and "Is it like seeing the 'actual' object that caused me harm or only an abstract image of that object?"

When we think about our suffering, it is usually overwhelming. If we can begin to recognize that the appearing object is just a generality—a projection—our suffering will naturally decrease. This type of investigation is a powerful way to cut through our projections and the suffering they cause.

Next, think about your brain. Most of us believe that this organ is where our mind is situated. Look at whatever specifically characterized phenomena you find in the area where you think your brain is located. What are they like? What do they have in common with this famous "gray matter"? Look at the thoughts that are supposedly produced by the brain. Do they come out of some organic structure? What part of the brain do they come from? Do they come from the front? The back? Can you find the generally characterized phenomenon called "brain"? What is that like?

We are very attached to scientific models of materiality—brains, elements, light waves, subatomic particles, DNA—all of these seem to exist "from their own side." However, when we investigate to see what we actually perceive, we can't find any specific characteristics that correspond to these conceptual models. In particular, "the brain" is a powerful concept that obscures our experience of mind.

At this point, it is important to recall that concepts are not useless and we do not have to get rid of them. There are lots of things you can't do without concepts: find your way around the city, fly airplanes, discover new medicines, improve crop yields, or teach and learn about the dharma. The Sutra school not only distinguishes between perception and conception, it also makes a detailed study of *inferential valid cognition*, which explains the qualities of correct and incorrect conceptions. From this perspective, it is clear that the problem with concepts is not the concepts—it is our confusion about them. We do not see concepts clearly, accurately, just as they are.

Sautrantika investigations unravel our confusion about the appearance of perception and conception. This school says that specifically characterized phenomena are genuinely real, they are able to perform functions. Direct experience of the tall buildings in New York City is genuine reality. On the other hand, generally characterized phenomena only appear to be real; they do not perform functions. You can't rent an office in your mental image of New York's tall buildings.

Dharmakirti describes the view of the Sutra school in his *Commentary on Valid Cognition* as follows:

> Here, what is genuinely able to perform a function
> Is what genuinely exists.
> Everything else is seemingly existent.
> These are explained as specifically characterized and
>   generally characterized phenomena.[3]

A POETIC INTERLUDE

W HAT DOES THE SUTRA school's genuine reality look like? It is our ordinary experience stripped of all conceptions. Because specifically characterized phenomena are inexpressible—as we saw when we talked about the taste of candy—you can't really describe the experience. However, when you have the experience, you can express something that gives another person a feeling for that experience. Artistic expressions can be a very good way to evoke the experience of the inexpressible. There are many contemplative arts, or dharma arts, that do just this.

As Chögyam Trungpa describes it:

> The whole philosophy of dharma art is that you don't try to be artistic, but you just approach objects as they are and the message comes through automatically. It is like Japanese flower arranging. You don't try to be artistic; you just chop off certain twigs and branches that seem to be out of line with the flow. Then you put the twigs in the container and the flowers underneath, and it automatically becomes a whole landscape.[1]

Japanese haiku often seem to capture the flavor of genuine reality in ways that are harmonious with the Sutra school's view. Here are a few haiku from a lovely collection called *The Essential Haiku: Versions of Bashō, Buson, and Issa*. These poems are

beautifully translated and edited by Robert Hass, who was the
poet laureate of the United States from 1995 to 1997.

Matsuo Basho (1644–1694)

It's not like anything
they compare it to —
 the summer moon.

❧

Wrapping the rice cakes,
with one hand
 she fingers back her hair.

❧

Heat waves shimmering
one or two inches
 above the dead grass.

❧

Fleas, lice,
a horse peeing
 near my pillow.

❧

Lightning —
and in the dark
 the screech of a night heron.[2]

❧

YOSA BUSON (1716–1783)

They end their flight
one by one —
　　crows at dusk.

Blow of an ax,
pine scent,
　　the winter woods.

Lighting the lantern —
the yellow chrysanthemums
　　lose their color.

A tethered horse,
snow
　　in both stirrups.[3]

KOBAYASHI ISSA (1763–1827)

Nursing her child
the mother
　　counts its fleabites.

Washing the saucepans—
the moon glows on her hands
in the shallow river.

§

These sea slugs,
they just don't seem
Japanese.[4]

7
MAHAYANA 101

MUCH AS GREAT SHIPS crossing the international dateline hold celebrations and initiatory rites for their passengers and crews, the haiku provide a marker and celebration for our passage from the views of the hinayana schools to those of the mahayana.

Crossing the dateline is an excellent opportunity to realize that time is illusory: one minute it is Tuesday and the next it is Monday. Likewise, the passage from the hinayana to the mahayana is when we might see that, like time itself, all phenomena are illusory. This passage is where we decisively part company with the way worldly people normally see things. We usually think the world is real and substantial. It appears that way to us, and our experience seems to confirm that it really is that way. The mahayana teachings radically challenge this understanding.

All mahayana schools show that there is no world outside that exists the way we conceive it to be. Outer and inner worlds are projections. On the other hand, no school denies that there are appearances, but appearances are no longer taken to be the appearances of real objects. They are empty of any true existence. Relatively they appear, but ultimately they have no nature.

Our beliefs in materiality, or true existence, are visceral and extremely deeply rooted. When these beliefs are challenged, it threatens the very fabric of ego, and when ego is threatened, it will marshal a vast array of emotionality and conceptuality to its defense. This happens because, seeing there is no material basis to this world, we understand that the ego has no material basis either. Even a hint of this understanding provokes a strong reaction. Among many other possible reactions, this can take the form of anger, which ridicules mahayana views; passion, which takes these views as new intellectual playthings; or ignorance, which does not let the meaning of these teachings penetrate.

I have a good friend who has devoted more than two decades of his life to Buddhist practice and study. When he encounters mahayana teachings on essencelessness (particularly the Mind Only view), it makes him crazy. He recently told me that for twenty years he has been obsessed with proving that there must be some material basis for phenomena. Every time he hears a teacher present teachings about these views, he is compelled to ask a variant of the same, often highly elaborated question to try to show that there must be something underlying the things we experience. Whenever his friends see him raise his hand at a talk, we think, "Here comes 'The Question.'" To his chagrin, the answer is invariably that there is no such basis—usually delivered with a big smile.

Two Types of Egolessness

The Sanskrit term *hinayana* is often translated as "lesser vehicle," but it can also be translated as "narrow vehicle." It is "narrow" in the sense of being focused; the hinayana is focused on ending suffering. Because of this, the hinayana is also referred to as the vehicle of *individual liberation*.

Suffering is eliminated by recognizing that the ego or self is just imputed to exist and that it is actually our thoughts that do this. The self is a projection. It is only apparently real and can't be found upon investigation. This is called "seeing the selflessness, or egolessness, of the individual." Seeing that ego is illusory, the poisons and karmic actions arising from ego collapse, and freedom from suffering is achieved. Whether phenomena truly exist or not isn't much of an issue for hinayanists.

The term *mahayana* means "vast vehicle." The mahayana is vast because it has the vast aim of the complete liberation of all sentient beings. To accomplish complete liberation, we need to recognize not only the selflessness of the individual but also the *selflessness of all phenomena*. It is not enough to recognize the selflessness of the individual and give up the poisons and karmic actions. This *does* lead to the cessation of suffering, but mahayanists consider this a temporary state because it still contains ignorance. Genuine reality has not yet been recognized. It is obscured by the clinging that takes outer and inner phenomena to be real. To put it very simply, selflessness of the individual is realized when we see that the skandhas are not a self. However, we still need stable certainty that the skandhas themselves are illusory.

While mahayana schools differ in the ways they uncover genuine reality (and in the subtlety of their explanations), all of them emphasize conduct that is in harmony with the realization of egolessness—namely, the cultivation of loving-kindness and compassion.

PROPONENTS OF TRULY EXISTENT THINGS

As we have seen in previous chapters, both Vaibhashikas and Sautrantikas understand that apparent reality (particularly the self) is fabricated by mind. Vaibhashikas say that coarse objects and durations of consciousness only seem to exist—that is, they are just concepts. Sautrantikas explain that what only seems to exist are generally characterized phenomena: the abstract images that appear to our thoughts.

On the other hand, both of these schools believe that there is a material basis for genuine reality. Because of this, they are sometimes referred to as the "proponents of truly existent things." Vaibhashikas say that what is genuinely real are minute particles of matter and subtle moments of consciousness. They say that these *indivisible*, or *partless, particles* and *irreducible moments of consciousness* really exist as substances.

Sautrantikas also assert subtle particles, but they qualify that by saying that these particles cannot be perceived directly. They believe that we perceive *aspects* of these particles, which they consider to be *hidden objects*. They say that what is genuinely real are the specifically characterized phenomena based on these hidden objects, the hidden objects themselves, and the minds perceiving them. For Vaibhashikas and Sautrantikas, both mind and matter are substantial.

Mahayanists show that the hinayana schools don't take their analysis far enough. They cling to material bases for phenomena even though the material bases they propose are—just like the self—fabricated by mind. Partless particles and irreducible moments of consciousness are concepts used to explain the phenomena we experience. They are not verifiable by experience itself. Upon investigation, no such bases can be found.

To point out the nonexistence of partless particles, mahayanists show that they are not logical. Suppose, for example, a partless particle was encircled by four other partless particles in the four cardinal directions. If the part of the central particle that is touching or facing the particle on the eastern side does not also touch or face the particle on the western side, then the central particle would, in fact, have parts. If it does touch or face both the eastern and the western particles, it would not occupy any space, and a collection of such particles would also not occupy any space, in which case gross forms would be impossible. Therefore, it must have parts. Partless particles are just mental constructs.

A similar method is used to show that irreducible moments of consciousness cannot exist. For example, suppose that the present is an irreducible, partless moment. This present moment must be connected to the past and also connected to the future. If the connection between present and past is the same as the connection between present and future, then the past and the future would be directly connected and the present would not have any time at all. If the connection between the present and the future is not the same as the connection between the present and the past, they are different connections so there must be two present moments! Therefore, irreducible moments of consciousness are also just mental constructs.

WESTERN SCIENCE

It is not too hard to see through ancient theories about matter and time. It is a lot harder to see through the views of the current ethos. We live in an age that is dominated by the scientific endeavor, and our thinking is permeated with scientific ideas in both crude and sophisticated ways. Many of these concepts appear to support our instinctive feelings that things really exist, so we need to investigate them to see if this is so.

During my lifetime, Western science has presented a succession of concepts about the basic building blocks of matter. Scientists have put forward a succession of increasingly subtle particles as bases for the phenomena we perceive. From my childhood in the 1950s and '60s, I remember pictures of tiny spheres in elliptical orbits around larger spheres that were supposed to represent the electrons, protons, and neutrons forming the atom. At that time, these were regarded as the basic constituents of the universe. By the early sixties, we were looking at pictures of Nobel Prize winners Watson and Crick posing with large models (which might have been made out of Ping-Pong balls) that represented the way atoms combined to form the structure of the DNA molecule. Later on, we heard about quantum mechanics and Heisenberg's uncertainty principle, and it became hard to know whether the particles we had come to depend on should be visualized as spheres or waves or something more abstract.

Around the time I left college, we started hearing that there were even more fundamental particles called quarks, which came in funny "flavors" with names like "charm" and "strange." Over the next decade, quarks were joined by more particles, called leptons, and a new Standard Model of matter emerged.

Recently, we have been hearing about even more subtle particles as physicists unveil what is sometimes hailed as the new "Theory of Everything"—the string theory. The string theory tells us that when we are able to examine our quarks, leptons, and other particles even more precisely, we will find that each of these is not really pointlike, but consists of tiny, one-dimensional loops, like infinitely thin rubber bands. These vibrating, oscillating, dancing filaments are called "string." Now, that is something to visualize!

From a mahayana perspective, it is safe to say that Western science will never get to the bottom of this—it will never discover fundamental building blocks—because the very notion of fundamental building blocks is based on the belief that phenomena truly exist and that therefore some basic unit of phenomena must exist. Yet, whatever basic unit science proposes will inevitably be just a theoretical construct, a concept, and will eventually be divisible into smaller constructs when the theoretical tools and experimental technology become available. It is like the story that Stephen Hawking tells in *A Brief History of Time*:

> A well-known scientist (some say it was Bertrand Russell) once gave a public lecture on astronomy. He described how the earth orbits around the sun and how the sun, in turn, orbits around the centre of a vast collection of stars called our galaxy. At the end of the lecture, a little old lady at the back of the room got up and said: "What you have told us is rubbish. The world is really a flat plate supported

on the back of a giant tortoise." The scientist gave a superior smile before replying, "What is the tortoise standing on?" "You're very clever, young man, very clever," said the old lady. "But it's turtles all the way down."[1]

Rather than finding fundamental building blocks, science will continue to find subtler particles "all the way down."

PUSHING STRING

The images that scientists and textbook writers use to explain their efforts make the imperceptible seem tangible. I have recounted a few of the particle images that stick with me. No doubt you have your own collection. It is commonly believed, both by scientists and the general public, that the world really is the way it is explained to be by scientific statements: things like quarks, leptons, and string actually exist. We may not be able to see them, but they are really there. They exist independently of the minds of the scientists whose theories and experiments create the models. This view is sometimes called *scientific realism.*

Scientific realism is deceptive because it mistakes concepts for things. This is not only the mahayana point of view but also the perspective of many Western philosophers who study the philosophy of science, and of many scientists themselves. Scientific models attempt to explain complex sets of observations with simpler sets of mathematical and/or verbal concepts. This is called *reductionism,* which is a cornerstone of scientific method. When these models are well grounded in observation, the concepts produce powerful and useful predictions, much as bus schedules predict how long you might have to wait for a No. 9 bus. The models are not "things" that make the predictions happen, any more than the bus schedule makes the bus come.

To see this, we can look at some comments from a contemporary scientist working on the frontiers of particle physics. David

Gross shared a Nobel Prize in Physics in 2004 for his work on string theory. Here is part of what he said about this theory in a recent interview:

> One of the strangest aspects of where we are in string theory after 35 years is that we don't really know what string theory is. There are all these people working on string theory and doing wonderful things, sometimes answering old problems, sometimes coming up with new scenarios. But if you really ask them, "What is string theory?" they'll give you a glib remark, a glib description, and describe certain of its aspects. If you ask them again, "What is string theory?" if they're honest they'll say, "Well, we don't know." We have this incredibly powerful set of tools and methods that describe this intellectual structure, and yet we really don't know what lies at the core of that, what the unifying principles are, what the theory actually is that has all of these different aspects that we can partially describe.[2]

This quotation makes it clear that scientific theory is an "intellectual structure." It is only our imagination that transforms this into material objects. Here is an investigation that might clarify this. You can do this with your eyes either open or closed, but in either case, when the investigation says "look," do this with your mind's eye, not your organ of sight.

Let your mind rest a little, and then look at what you conceive your world to be. Slowly look in front and in back. Look to either side and above and below. When you are not using your eyes to see, what do you notice? Are there familiar landmarks around you? What about in the distance? Look again.

Ask yourself what these objects are made of. Are they made of particles like atoms, quarks, and string? Are they made of mental imagery? Investigate this well.

THE MIND-BODY PROBLEM

We can approach the same issues from a different angle by asking what is the relationship between mind and body; or in other words, what is the relationship between mind and matter? We touched on this briefly in chapter 4, and now we will look at it in a slightly different fashion.

The mind-body problem is quite familiar to Western philosophers and neuroscientists. Put simply, the issue is: Are mind and body two different substances? Is one of them reducible to the other? Or is there still another possible relationship between these two?

The first view, that mind and body are two completely different substances is known as *dualism*. This is our usual way of thinking about the world. Mind perceives a physical world "out there" that is different from it. There is a fundamental problem with this explanation: how do physical objects "out there" get into mind "in here"? We only know about objects because they are experienced. We can theorize that physical objects are the basis for our experience, but how can we ever know them directly? Experience is always mental—that's what mind does. How can we separate the object from our experience? This is a very good subject to investigate.

Look at different objects. Can you find a point where the object stops and the mind begins? What is the interface between the physical and the mental? Is it made of mind or is it made of matter? Can you see how physical objects become mental experience?

The problems with dualism cause many scientists to take the view that there can't be two different substances—everything must be reducible to just the physical. This view is known as *materialism* or *physicalism*. The only substance is matter. This view leads to the assumption that experience can be completely explained by mapping mind's material basis, the neural correlates of mental events. The Holy Grail for many neuroscientists is to discover neural correlates for consciousness itself. The problem with this view is that it does not begin to explain how purely material substances can give rise to subjective experience. Here is the way philosopher David Chalmers describes the issue:

> There is not just one problem of consciousness. "Consciousness" is an ambiguous term, referring to many different phenomena. Each of these phenomena needs to be explained, but some are easier to explain than others. At the start, it is useful to divide the associated problems of consciousness into "hard" and "easy" problems. The easy problems of consciousness are those that seem directly susceptible to the standard methods of cognitive science, whereby a phenomenon is explained in terms of computational or neural mechanisms. The hard problems are those that seem to resist those methods. . . .
>
> The really hard problem of consciousness is the problem of experience. When we think and perceive, there is a whir of information-processing, but there is also a subjective aspect. . . . This subjective aspect is experience. When we see, for example, we experience visual sensations: the felt quality of redness, the experience of dark and light, the quality of depth in a visual field. Other experiences go

along with perception in different modalities: the sound of a clarinet, the smell of mothballs. Then there are bodily sensations, from pains to orgasms; mental images that are conjured up internally; the felt quality of emotion, and the experience of a stream of conscious thought.[3]

Since subjective experience is the most intimate aspect of our entire existence, it is hard to take seriously any solution to the mind-body problem that ignores it. Here is a way to contemplate this:

What is the knowing quality of mind like? Is it a thing? Could it be the product of a chemical soup or a biological stew? If there is only matter, wouldn't inanimate objects, such as stones and trees, also have subjective experience?

Here are some interesting comments on this subject from His Holiness the Dalai Lama from his book *The Art of Happiness* that provide another good contemplation:

The Western approach differs in some respects from the Buddhist approach. Underlying all Western modes of analysis is a very strong rationalistic tendency—an assumption that everything can be accounted for. And on top of that, there are constraints created by certain premises that are taken for granted. For example, recently I met with some doctors at a university medical school. They were talking about the brain and stated that thoughts and feelings were the result of different chemical reactions and changes in the brain. So, I raised the question: is it possible to conceive the reverse sequence, where the thought gives rise to the sequence of chemical events in the brain? However, the part that I found most interesting was the answer that the scientist gave. He said, "We start from the premise that all thoughts are products or functions of chemical reactions in the brain." So it is simply a kind of rigidity, a decision not to challenge their own way of thinking. . . .

"I think that in modern Western society, there seems to be a powerful cultural conditioning that is based on science. But in some instances, the basic premises and parameters set up by Western science can limit your ability to deal with certain realities. . . .

"It's a bit like you've lost something and you decide that the object is in this room. And once you have decided this, then you've already fixed your parameters; you've precluded the possibility of its being outside the room or in another room. So you keep on searching and searching, but you are not finding it, yet you continue to assume that it is still hidden somewhere in the room!"[4]

Dualism and materialism are the alternatives that assert a material basis for a world "out there." Clearly there are problems with both positions. There are two alternative possibilities to consider. The first is that everything must be reducible to mind. This view is known as *idealism* in Western philosophy, and Mind Only in Buddhism. We will look at the Mind Only school's view in the next chapter. The last possibility is that everything is ultimately neither mind nor matter, because neither mind nor matter ultimately exists—mind and matter are dependently arisen mere appearances. This is the position of the Middle Way schools, which we will discuss beginning in chapter 10.

In Defense of Science

You might conclude from the above that a modern mahayanist would be anti-science. *Au contraire*. The physical and biological sciences (along with their first cousin, technology) have made amazing contributions to the longevity, leisure, comfort, and entertainment of a great many of us in developed areas, and potentially to many more throughout the planet. I am personally happy to live in a house with electric heat; I like working on my iMac, driving my car around town, and flying around the world; I am eager to take Western medicine when I am ill, and am quite content to eat French asparagus in winter and New Zealand apples year-round.

The pillars of the scientific method—empirical observation, reductionism, and logical reasoning—are powerful tools to help people understand and manipulate the cause-and-effect relationships of apparent reality (which Buddhists call interdependence). These manipulations bring both benefit and harm.

Instead of rejecting science, I have tried to show some of its limits. Scientific realism is based on a naive understanding of what science actually tells us. In fact, many scientists are not scientific realists who believe their enterprise describes a freestanding objective reality. There are more than a few mahayana Buddhist scientists today. It is also naive, as the Dalai Lama points out, to think that everything can be accounted for in materialistic terms, the belief that everything can be reduced to "the machine." Unfortunately, these materialist views can prevent us from understanding the causal relationships that are most important to us: the determinants of happiness and sorrow, bondage and liberation.

THE SCIENCE OF MIND

The tools that form the basis for Western science are also the tools the Buddha used to explore and explain the science of the mind, which does address these issues. While Buddhism is often thought of as a path of faith, it is also a path of reason. The Buddhist teachings show us what types of actions cause happiness and what types cause suffering. They unlock the door to liberation by providing methods for abandoning clinging to all concepts about apparent reality, which obscure the inexpressible dynamic display of genuine reality.

Here is a quotation from Ponlop Rinpoche, from a talk called "A Science of Mind" that makes a good contemplation:

Buddhism is a journey into the depths of one's heart and mind, the inner reality of one's essence, an exploration of who we are and what we are. This spiritual journey is nothing more and nothing less than discovering this inner reality.

Buddhist spiritual teachings present a genuine science of mind that allows one to uncover this inner reality, the nature of the mind and the phenomena that our minds experience. When we say that Buddhism is a "science," we do not mean the dry science of analyzing material things. We are talking about something much deeper. We are talking about going into the depths of the reality of our inner world, which is the most powerful world.

The teachings of Lord Buddha Shakyamuni, which we often refer to by the Sanskrit term buddhadharma, set forth a path that frees one from disturbing emotions and fundamental ignorance. This dharma frees us from existence in samsara, defined by samsaric fear, and leads us towards the fruition of independence, the fruition of the state of complete freedom, the state of fearlessness, going beyond fear.

By closely looking at buddhadharma, or Buddhism, we thus find that it is a pure path, pure teachings, a pure science, a science of mind. In this sense, Buddhist spirituality is not what is ordinarily meant by the term "religion." It is rather closer to a humanistic science, a pure and genuine philosophy of humanity and science which works with the two sides of our samsaric mind, the negative aspect and the positive aspect of our mind. Fundamentally it is the science of working with the very basic nature of our mind.[5]

And as Khenpo Tsültrim Gyamtso wrote in his aspiration "Auspiciousness That Lights Up the Universe":

May the sciences that explore outside
Be joined with the inner science of the mind
To excellently put an end
To mistaken views and confusion
And by this may auspiciousness
Light up the whole universe![6]

8

CHITTAMATRA
There Is Only Mind

THE TWO MAIN BRANCHES of the mahayana are the Chittamatra, or Mind Only school, and the Madhyamaka, or
Middle Way school. In this chapter we will begin to explore the
view and methods of the Chittamatra school. This school is also
known as the Yogachara, Yoga Practice, or Yogic Conduct, school,
because its view is deeply grounded in the practice of meditation.
Noble Asanga, the fourth-century master who first widely propa-
gated these teachings, meditated on Lord Maitreya, the tenth-
bhumi bodhisattva and regent of Buddha Shakyamuni, for twelve
years in solitary retreat. After overcoming incredible difficulties
and despair, Asanga finally beheld Maitreya face-to-face and
received many teachings from him, including those known as the
Five Treatises of Maitreya. These texts present extensive teachings
on the mahayana, and in particular, the core teachings of Chittamatra.

To briefly summarize these teachings, Yogacarins see that all
phenomena are nothing other than mind. They see that all conceptions are mind, and all perceptions are also mind. Our worlds
are made of mind in the same way that dream worlds are made

of mind. This is not an understanding based on inference or assumption. They realize this directly in meditation.

They also see that the perceiver of phenomena is nothing other than mind. Perceiver and perceived are not two different substances. There is no difference or separation between them. The duality that we normally experience is mistaken. It only appears when there is confusion.

Finally, they see that what truly exists is nondual self-awareness, which is the true nature of mind. The Mind Only system explains that this nondual self-awareness is genuine reality. Jamgön Kongtrül summarizes the Chittamatra view in *The Treasury of Knowledge* like this:

> Perceived objects and perceiving subjects' duality is
> relative.
> Consciousness that is empty of duality is genuine.
> This is the presentation of the mind-only school.[1]

The proposition that everything is mind is certainly counter-intuitive. It seems obvious that matter and mind are different things (just as it seems obvious that the self exists). Ego is allergic to groundlessness of any kind and is extraordinarily resourceful in reestablishing its ground. It is important to acknowledge any doubts you might have about the Mind Only view right at the beginning. If you don't, ego might end up paying lip service to this view to avoid letting it really penetrate.

The best way to approach the Mind Only view at the outset is to find examples of things you can easily see are only mind, even though they normally are considered material. You can expand your explorations from there. If you try to start with the things that provoke the most resistance, such as "You think getting run over by a car is just mind!" you probably won't get very far.

You might start by remembering how many realms you churn up in an hour of formless meditation, or recall the images of a vivid dream, to get a feeling for how powerful a creator mind is. Other examples that are helpful at the beginning are what seem to arise as "the three times"—past, present, and future. It is relatively easy to see that everything in the future is mind, because none of it has happened yet. How could next year be made of anything else? It is also fairly easy to see that since the past is gone, it must also be mind. Where else could it be? You might think that you could go back to someplace that you have been before, such as the place you were born, and that you would be returning to the past. But it would not be that past place. It would be the present. It is only thought that mistakes it for an "earlier" place.

Novels are another good example of mind-created worlds. Good literature gives you a vivid feeling of being in another environment, with people who seem to "come to life." It is only words printed on a page, but we can spend hours engrossed in these mental worlds.

Dreams are the best examples of mind-created worlds. Most of us find it very difficult to recognize dreams while we are dreaming. The dream contents seem completely real to us, as long as we are dreaming, but as soon as we wake up, it is easy to understand that dream contents are only mind.

Here are some quotations to help you penetrate the Mind Only view. The first one, from the *Buddhavatamsaka Sutra*, simply states the premise, but because it is the words of the Buddha, it shows that this view is based on his teachings:

The three realms of existence are merely mind.[2]

Next is a verse you can contemplate from *The Compendium of the Essence of Wisdom*, quoted by Jamgön Kongtrül in *The Treasury of Knowledge*:

That which has parts does not exist.
Subtle particles also are not existent.
Appearances apart from mind cannot be observed.
Experiences are like dreams.
Consciousness free from perceiver and perceived
Exists in genuine actuality.
So proclaim those who have gone
To the far shore of the ocean of the Yogic Conduct
    texts.[3]

Finally, here is a paragraph to contemplate from a description of the six realms of samsara from Chögyam Trungpa's *Transcending Madness*:

Strangely enough, these experiences of the six realms—gods, jealous gods, human beings, animals, hungry ghosts, and hell—are *space*, different versions of space. It seems intense and solid, but in actual fact it isn't at all. They are different aspects of space—that's the exciting or interesting part. In fact, it is complete open space, without any colors or any particularly solid way of relating. That is why they have been described as six types of consciousness. It is pure consciousness rather than a solid situation. . . . That is why these levels are referred to as *loka*, which means "realm" or "world."[4]

THERE IS ONLY MIND BECAUSE . . .

These examples provide glimpses of the way mind can appear as outer objects, but we need to investigate further to gain confidence in this view. One of the most powerful reasons supporting the Chittamatrin view is that the *only* way to know that things exist is that they appear to mind. Khenchen Thrangu Rinpoche explains this nicely in his commentary on Maitreya's *Distinguishing Dharma and Dharmata:**

> If we consider various external phenomena such as a mountain, a chair, or a thimble, we feel that the object exists. We do this because we can see it. It is merely the seeing of something that leads us to feel, think and believe that it exists. There is no other way to prove the existence of something. For instance, if we think that a particular mountain exists, we say, "Well, I saw it and that's why I think so." If we ask someone else, "Why do you think that such a thing exists?" All they can answer is, "Well, I saw it. That's all." It's just an appearance for one's mind. Consider the stupa outside this monastery. We think it exists. Why do we think that it exists? We believe this because we see it. We see it because it appears to our mind. There is no way to demonstrate the existence of something that has not appeared to our mind. There is no way to demonstrate the existence of something without its appearing to mind. Therefore, external phenomena and internal mind are inseparable.
>
> Similarly, if we hear a sound, we think that the sound exists. Why do we think the sound exists? "Because I heard it," is our answer. Is there an unheard sound? No there isn't. Thus, whether we talk about visible images, sounds that are apprehended by our ear, smells apprehended by our nose, or various tastes that are tasted by our tongue, it is only because of their appearing to our mind that we think they exist. Thus, external things are just internal mind. Therefore, these external appearances are just our internal mind. They are not truly established as what they appear to be.[5]

---

* The title of this text has also been translated as *Distinguishing Phenomena from Pure Being.*

You might still think that things appearing to mind are separate from the mind itself, but how could that be? It doesn't make sense to think that a thing and its appearance are different—like a cat and a dog. How could you prove that there is anything behind the appearance itself?

You might try to challenge this by saying that we can prove that external things exist even if we can't directly perceive them. "We use instruments to do this and we use inferences to do this." One response to this is that the instruments appear to mind, the inferential logic appears to mind, and the images of the things that are supposedly "proven to exist" also appear to mind.

You might take a different tack by arguing that external objects must exist because they are experienced by many people in the same way. I will paraphrase Mipham Gyamtso's eloquent response to this objection from his commentary on Maitreya's *Distinguishing Phenomena and Pure Being*.[6]

Superficially, there appear to be objects that are experienced in common. However, upon examination you find they do not exist. The things that are claimed to be observed in common are only similar subjective experiences of different mindstreams. The fact that these appearances are private impressions of mindstreams that differ from each other proves that they could never be established as truly common experience. To say that there is an external object that is something other than these impressions can't be correct. That would be an object that doesn't appear to any mind.

The similarity of the appearances is due to the similar karma or history of the beings perceiving them. When you carefully examine what is thought to be common experience, even though the appearances may be similar, that does not show that they are caused by outer objects. For example, people will see similar appearances watching an illusion, without the object being there. In the same way, beings with similar habitual tendencies will experience similar environments until those habitual tendencies have been exhausted, but these are not caused by existing outer objects.

This is something we need to contemplate to understand. We can do that using the root verse that Mipham was commenting upon:

> What appear to be outer, perceivable in common,
> Are perceiving awareness; they are not referents
> Existing as something extrinsic to consciousness,
> Because they are only experienced as common.[7]

Perhaps these arguments seem too abstract or theoretical to you. But we can look at some tangible examples to show how commonly perceived external objects do not really exist.

PRESIDENT GEORGE W. BUSH

As of this writing, George W. Bush is perceived to be a good leader by many people. Many others perceive him to be a dangerous idiot and a tool of corporate interests. On the other hand, his daughters perceive him as a father. His parents perceive him as a son. Osama bin Laden sees George W. Bush as an enemy and a demon. To a mosquito, George W. Bush is a meal. The microorganisms that inhabit his intestines perceive him as a home. Whose version is right? Each being believes that what they think they see when they look at the object we call George W. Bush is real. Even the idea of there being an object there at all is just a concept, for any object that existed separate from mind could not be known by mind at all.

To make matters worse, George thinks of himself as "me," while we think of George as "him" (unless we are talking directly to him, in which case he becomes "you" or "Mr. President").

If we look more closely at this situation, we might find that we usually see George W. Bush on television or in the newspapers, and what we perceive is not a person at all but just a lot of colored light emitted from a screen or many dots of ink on a piece of paper.

This example demonstrates that what we think of as external objects are just our projected concepts. Each of us is experiencing our own projections. There is nothing "out there" with the characteristics we imagine. This is not only important for understanding the view of the Mind Only school, it has great practical significance. So much of our suffering comes from believing that our projections really exist the way we perceive them, particularly our projections about other people and what they have, or have not, done to us. Even a glimmer of understanding that these projections are only mind will make our pain diminish—not to mention the transformative effect recognizing this directly will have.

Here is another quotation from Mipham Gyamtso that you can contemplate on this subject:

> When you see someone as an enemy and they die, you
>   are happy,
> When you see someone as a friend and they die, you
>   are sad.
> Happiness and suffering never exist in the entity itself.[8]

ASK MR. FLY

One of the more powerful methods that I know for undermining our belief that things really are the way we see them is the Ask Mr. Fly test. To use this test, you need to know a little about a fly's visual system. If you have ever gotten a close look at a fly's head, you know that their eyes are quite large, and quite different from our own. They are called "compound" eyes because they are made up of many divisions or facets.

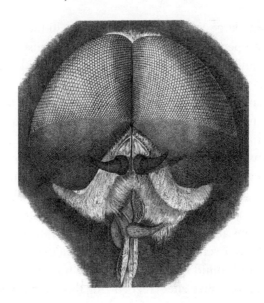

In this drawing you can see the individual facets of the eye. A fly's eyes are very good at detecting motion (as you can tell when you try to catch one), but they do not see shapes very clearly. Because each one of the facets has its own lens, the image processed by the eye is like a mosaic. Flies can perceive colors, but not in the same range we perceive. They see blue, ultraviolet, green, and yellow, but they do not see red.

Armed with these factoids, it is easy to use the Ask Mr. Fly test. Begin by looking at something familiar, such as this book, and ask yourself, "What would this look like to a fly?" Take some time to imagine this. Obviously, it would look a lot different from the way it looks to you. Then reflect on the following questions:

Do I see this object correctly? Does the fly see it correctly? Does the fly see a poorer image of the book because of its inferior visual system?

If you believe that your version of the book is the correct one, what makes you say that it is more valid than Mr. Fly's version? Imagine looking at cars and houses and people through a fly's eyes. Since there is no ideal observer, there is no objective basis for what things look like. All appearances depend on the consciousness observing them. By the way, if you really don't like flies, you can use the Ask Mrs. Fish test instead.

EXPLAINING APPEARANCES

If appearances are not produced by objects, how does the Mind Only school explain the fact that they do appear? The explanation is that experiences leave imprints or traces in the part of our mind called the all-basis or base consciousness (the *alayavijnana* in Sanskrit). These imprints or traces are like seeds. The Mind Only school says that by the power of *vasana* (another Sanskrit term that is variously translated as "habitual patterns," "latencies," "karmic tendencies," "karmic impressions," "habitual tendencies," or "instincts"), these traces ripen as our present experience.

What is this all-basis consciousness like? Jamgön Kongtrül explains (calling it "the appropriating consciousness," because it appropriates all traces) in *The Treasury of Knowledge*:

The reasons that the alaya exists are given in the *Sutra Unraveling the Intention*:

The appropriating consciousness, profound and subtle,
flows with its seeds, like a river.
It is wrong to regard it as a self;
thus I do not teach it to the immature.

The characteristics of the alaya are as described in the *Abhidharma Sutra*:

The expanse of beginningless time
is the source of all phenomena.
Since it exists, there are beings
and the attainment of nirvana.

Since the alaya consciousness, on the basis of the habitual tendencies for all afflictive phenomena, holds the
seeds for such phenomena, it is the cause for the arising of
all afflictive phenomena. Since it can become anything, it
is also not obscured. It is indeterminate, because it is neither virtuous nor unvirtuous.[9]

In other words, our current experiences arise through the
interactions of the mental imprints of our previous experiences
that have accumulated from time without beginning. Here is the
way this process is described in the *Lankavatara Sutra*:

The mind stirred by habitual tendencies
Arises as outer appearances.
They are not existent objects but mind itself.
To see external objects is mistaken.[10]

This might not seem like a convincing explanation for the
trees, computers, and people that we regularly experience. You
might well wonder how such stable, detailed appearances could
be caused by habitual patterns. Why do all the things in the world
seem to fit together if they are just our habits? Habitual patterns,
karmic tendencies, and instincts seem much too vague to
account for this. We know that we might have a habitual pattern
for reading the newspaper in the morning, or for brushing our
teeth after every meal. We might believe in a tendency toward
eating midnight snacks, or an instinct for being generous, but
habitual tendencies for producing the appearances of cities and
television shows seems very far-fetched.

In fact we have many habitual tendencies that are so stable and deeply ingrained that we don't even know they are just our habitual tendencies. Take, for example, what happens when we drive down the street where we live. We never have to think about which house is our home. We unerringly "know" which one it is, even if we have been away for months. How do we know this? From its own side, the house does not say, "I am your home!" Rather, it is our habitual pattern to see it as our home. When we move, without missing a beat, we will see it as our former home.

Here is another example. Think about your habitual tendencies for your native language. When you look at these strange shapes on the paper in front of you, sounds and meanings appear to your mind. For most of us, this is almost 100 percent effective and requires virtually no effort at all; yet there are no sounds, words, or meanings on the printed page. They don't exist externally at all. They are merely habitual patterns. If you reflect on the complexity and intricacy of language, with all its vocabulary, syntax, pronunciation, and grammar, you can see that thought and speech continually arise solely due to habitual tendencies. How much of a stretch is it to imagine that visible forms and sounds might arise in the same way? According to the Chittamatra school, this is exactly what happens.

You might still find this explanation unsatisfactory. This view is so radically different from conventional dualistic understanding and our deep-rooted dualistic habits that it is extremely difficult to wrap our minds around. If that is the case, then instead of asking, "How could all these objects really be only mind?" ask, "How could they not be mind?" As we saw earlier, even the tiniest particles of matter do not truly exist. Since there is no truly existent matter, then appearances must be mind. And since appearances are known by our mind, they must be of the same stuff as mind. If they were something fundamentally different, how could they ever be known?

No Duality

The first part of the Mind Only view is that there are no material objects, only mind. This leads us to the next part: that there is no duality between perceivers and what is perceived. We already know that these cannot be two different substances, but we need to investigate if there is still some separation between them.

Our usual way of experiencing the world is discursive: we tell ourselves (and others) what we are experiencing. The discursiveness and the projections that we think about seem to be located in different places—across from each other, or somehow separated from each other. Our thinking seems to be "in our head," and our emotions seem to be "in our heart," while the things we think about or have feelings toward seem to be some distance away. Much of the time, our consciousness is gathered in the location of our head or our heart and we feel like a caterpillar wrapped up in a cocoon. All of these give us a strong experiential sense of duality, and our usual way of thinking about the world confirms and reinforces these feelings.

But this is not the way it actually is. Discursiveness is not actually perceiving what it is reporting. If the thoughts were the perceivers, we would need to think about each thought in order to perceive what we were thinking! Then we would have to think about the thought that was thinking about the thought. This would be endless. Of course it is not that way.

The Mind Only school avoids this circular explanation by positing *self-awareness*. We can see that mind is self-aware—cognizant of itself—because we don't need to be told by someone else what we are experiencing. We know when we are happy and when we are sad. We know when we are thinking.

The Sakya Pandita explained the relationship of self-awareness to our sensory experience and our thinking in the following verse from *The Treasury of Pramana*:

Sense consciousness is a mute who can see;
Conceptual consciousness is blind, but chatters on.
Self-awareness has all faculties complete
And makes a connection between the two.[11]

The Sakya Pandita's explanation is very subtle and profound.
It is worth contemplating.

THE IMPORTANCE OF TAKING
THIS VIEW TO HEART

Why is all of this important? It is important because we are so
attached to the appearances of this life. We do not want to accept
that these appearances are no more substantial than dreams, and
they are all destined to dissolve when we die. Because of this, our
lives are strained and distorted, and when the time of death
comes, our anguish at losing these seemingly solid and enduring
reference points will be excruciating.

We can loosen our attachment to the appearances of this life
through listening, contemplating, and meditating. One of the
best ways to do this is to realize that the impermanence of all
things is directly connected to their insubstantiality. It is worthwhile reflecting on the impermanence of this life and its appearances. As the Buddha said:

Of all footprints, the elephant's are outstanding: just so, of
all subjects of meditation for a follower of the Buddhas, the
idea of impermanence is unsurpassed.[12]

And as the great Indian *siddha* Phadampa Sangye said:

At first, to be fully convinced of impermanence makes
you take up the Dharma; in the middle it whips up your

diligence; and in the end it brings you to the radiant dharmakaya.[13]

Finally, here is another quotation from Mipham Gyamtso about the importance of understanding this view:

> Those who strive on the path of both the sutras and the tantras must have a sure confidence in the understanding that all phenomena are but the self-experience or projection of the mind. There is nothing more important than this. During the night, when one is caught up in one's dreams, if one tries to deal with them using other methods, there is no end. But if one understands that they all arise from the mind itself, all are pacified at a single stroke. We should understand that the appearances of existence, which are endless in time and unlimited in extent, are similar to the visions of our dreams.[14]

9

THREE NATURES

To see things just as they are—what does that really mean? It means to see without delusion; to see clearly, without confusion. The Buddha taught that seeing things just as they are, we attain liberation, release—the final fruit of the path. Seeing things just as they are, we achieve deathlessness. This is the realization that while the appearances of this life arise and cease, basic mind is unceasing.

The Chittamatra school has a subtle and elegant way of explaining the delusion that prevents us from seeing things just as they are and the process of freeing ourselves from that delusion. They do this by distinguishing three aspects of experience, which they call "the three natures." In the previous chapter we explored the way this school establishes the view. In this chapter we will examine the three natures to help bring this view into our practice.

THE DEPENDENT NATURE

Nothing appears without cause. Whatever appears does so because of a complex set of causes and conditions. Ordinary worldly experience tells us this, and scientific theory and reasoning confirm it. Because appearances depend on causes and conditions, they are called "the dependent nature," or *paratantra* in Sanskrit. They are not independent. They are not under their own power. Because of this, they are sometimes called "the other-powered nature."

As we have discussed, the Mind Only school explains that appearances arise when the all-basis consciousness, or *alayavijnana*, is stirred by the power of habitual tendencies. Consciousnesses experiencing visible forms, sounds, smells, tastes, and bodily sensations arise due to traces, or predispositions, that have been deposited in the all-basis consciousness. It is through the power of these traces or predispositions that appearances are generated. What arises *depends* on these traces or predispositions; that is why they are called the "dependent" nature.

What is the nature or essence of the dependent nature? According to the Chittamatra school, it is luminous, knowing consciousness. What appears is the mind's luminosity, and what knows the appearances is also the mind's luminosity. They are not two separate entities.

THE IMAGINARY NATURE

When the mind's own luminosity is mistaken to be perceived objects and perceiving subjects, there is delusion. This is known as "the imaginary nature," or *parikalpita* in Sanskrit. These objects and perceivers are merely imputed by names, thoughts, and concepts. Because of this, they are sometimes called "the imputed nature." You could say that the objects that concepts and names refer to are the imaginary nature. These objects do not exist. They are imagined. Things that are not imputed by names and thoughts—things that are beyond names and concepts—are the dependent nature.

Thrangu Rinpoche describes the relationship between the dependent nature and the imaginary nature in his commentary on *Distinguishing the Middle from the Extremes* like this:

The dependent nature is the foundation for that which is imagined. The imagined nature is what one mistakenly takes the dependent nature to be; one apprehends and fixates upon it. Many sorts of dependent phenomena appear through the dependent relationship that is established by habitual tendencies which have existed within one's mind since the beginning of time and to which one has become very accustomed. Dependent appearances therefore occur and are taken to be something other than what they really are. It is like taking a reflection in a mirror to be the real object.[1]

THE PERFECTLY EXISTENT NATURE

That which is free from delusion, according to this system, is called "the perfectly existent nature," or the *parinishpanna* in Sanskrit, sometimes also called "the consummate nature" or "perfect reality." There are different ways of explaining the perfectly existent nature. In the Chittamatra system it is explained to be the dependent nature free of the imaginary nature.

To be free from the imaginary nature means to be free from the delusion of concept, free from the delusion of even the subtlest thought. Luminous knowing consciousness cannot be known by thought. No concept can describe it. Concepts cannot stick to it at all. What appears to thought is the imaginary nature. Therefore, the perfectly existent nature can only be realized through meditation.

APPLYING THE THREE NATURES

Because of their subtlety, the three natures can be described in a variety of ways. One way to summarize them would be to say that what is imagined by names, thoughts, and so on is the imaginary nature. What is not imagined by names and thoughts but appears due to causes and conditions is the dependent nature. The dependent nature's emptiness of the imaginary nature is the perfectly existent nature. This is a basic Chittamatra presentation. To make this clear, we will apply the three natures to different types of experience.

Let's say you encounter someone you know. The luminous knowing, or the mere appearance of that person, is the dependent nature. When you think, "This is a person. This is so-and-so," that is the imaginary nature. The concept "person" and the name are superimposed onto the mere appearance by thought. We project something imaginary onto mere appearance and blend these together as though appearance and concept were one thing. The dependent nature, empty of the imaginary nature, is the perfectly existent nature. That is what truly exists. We could look at the same situation in another way and say that the outward-facing aspect of the experience—the sense that there is a perceiver and something separate from it that is perceived—is the imaginary nature. It is a superimposition. There is no difference between perceiver and perceived, but our concepts imagine a difference. This difference is fabricated by thought. The perceived and perceiver's emptiness of being two is the perfectly existent nature.

We can apply the three natures to suffering in a similar way. Suffering itself is nothing other than luminous knowing. This is the dependent nature. The person suffering, the situation that brought about the suffering, and the idea that "suffering" is what is being experienced are the imaginary nature. The emptiness of that luminous-knowing feeling of the imaginary nature is the perfectly existent nature.

Now think about anger. The nature of anger is also luminosity—the dependent nature. The aspect of the anger that is directed outward is the imaginary nature. The object of the anger is also the imaginary nature. The anger's emptiness of what is imagined is the perfectly existent nature.

Another way to understand the three natures is to apply them to thoughts. Looking at thoughts this way, the thoughts themselves are the dependent nature because they are luminous knowing; the objects imputed by those thoughts are the imaginary nature; and the thoughts' emptiness of their objects is the perfectly existent nature.

In *The Treasury of Knowledge,* Jamgön Kongtrul shows how the three natures (called characteristics in this translation) can be connected with the Buddha's different ways of teaching:

> Consequently, in the sutras, teachings that list nonexistents are presentations of imagined characteristics. Teachings on illusions, dreams, mirages, and the like are about the dependent characteristic. The presentations of nonconceptuality and the unconditioned teach the consummate characteristic.[2]

We can bring the three natures into our practice in stages. Here is one way to go about it:

- First, to take the imaginary nature on the path, see that everything merely exists by imputation.
- Second, to take the dependent nature on the path, see that everything is merely consciousness.
- Third, to take the perfectly existent nature on the path, abandon any idea, including the idea that everything is merely consciousness.

NONEXISTENCE

The first step is to see that the objects of our thoughts are imaginary. When I think of you—the reader of this book—I am imagining something. When you think of me—the writer of this book—you are imagining something. If we don't know each other, that is the case; and if we do know each other, that is still the case.

The objects of thoughts seem to be real, and we think that they must be real, but they cannot be seen, they cannot be heard, they cannot be smelled, they cannot be tasted, and they cannot be touched. However we try to investigate them, they cannot be found. They have no substance. The thoughts appear, but their objects do not. At the very moment thoughts dawn, their objects are the imaginary nature.

We can explore this in meditation. Whatever practice you do can serve as a basis for this investigation as long as you balance the resting aspect of the practice with the looking aspect. When these aspects get out of balance, we get excited or depressed, heady or drowsy, and it is difficult to see anything clearly. An important skill to learn is to alternate resting and looking meditation so that the practice stays both fresh and grounded.

When you are somewhat settled in meditation, investigate to see if there is a connection between thoughts and their objects. What follows are suggestions you can experiment with. Please don't take them as some kind of system you need to stick with. They are more like clues to a treasure hunt.

Begin by mentally investigating your environment. First, try thinking of some of the local geography. No doubt images of the terrain will come to mind. When they do, try to see if these images are real terrain or imaginary terrain. Next, bring to mind things that seem to be behind you and investigate those in the same way. Are the things that are coming to mind what is actually behind your back or are they imaginary things? Do the same thing with what seems to be above and below and to the left and to the right of you. Bring to mind the town, city, or countryside you are in and investigate that as well.

In another session, do the same type of investigation for distant locations.

Think of the Eiffel Tower (unless you are lucky enough to be in Paris looking out at it, in which case you could think of the pyramids in Egypt instead). See if your image of the Eiffel Tower is connected with the actual Eiffel Tower.

At some point it should become clear that these places are merely imagined by thought, whether they are near or far. After that, when thoughts or images of places arise as you are meditating, recognize the imaginary nature of those places.

You can investigate the inhabitants of your environment in the same way.

Mentally look at friends and enemies, famous people and fictitious ones, to see if your thoughts connect with actual people, or are they imagined ones? What is the relationship of the image with an imagined object? Do they have any base or root? Look carefully at someone out of the corner of your eye to see how you fill in the picture with imagination. Look at situations of conflict and desire.

When you start to recognize the imaginary nature of these situations, they will start to lose their power over you, so this is a particularly important investigation.

Mentally look at what seem to be parts of yourself—
thoughts, visible forms, tactile sensations, emotions, and
all the rest. How do they connect up with that self? Can
you find a connection, or is the self also imaginary? Of
course you know the "correct" answer, but look beyond the
theory to see if the self really is imagined by thought.

The imaginary nature is pervasive. It is something you need to
investigate gradually. You can't take a plane to make this journey;
you need to go by foot. Sometimes there will be periods when
your mind won't settle. This might be caused by life situations,
what you had for breakfast, or just agitation caused by the investigations getting a little too close to home. You might be unable
to do this practice for a while. At those times, don't struggle or get
frustrated. Be kind to yourself and emphasize resting meditation
instead.

When you start to see that everything is merely imputed, it is
like recognizing you were dreaming as you are waking up: you
understand that the dream objects never existed. In the same
way, you see that all your thinking is thinking about what is imaginary. Usually, we believe that we need to get rid of thoughts
when we meditate, and we try to suppress them or cut them off.
But it is much better to see that what we are thinking about is
imaginary!

ILLUSIONS, DREAMS, AND MIRAGES

When we are experienced with the imaginary nature, we can
start to investigate the dependent nature. According to the Mind
Only school, the imaginary is what does not exist. The dependent is what does exist; it exists substantially—not as real objects—
but it actually does appear. Although it appears, it is merely

consciousness. We should explore this in meditation in the same way that we explored the imaginary nature.

Once your mind has settled a bit, look at visible forms by relaxing your gaze and seeing your whole visual field all at once. Relax into that. Usually we focus on visual highlights and think they are objects. Try to look without discursiveness and see visible form, free of objects. You might also notice that what is outside of the visual field does not appear at all.

In another session, do the same thing with sounds. When we do this, we usually hear sounds and immediately identify them with objects. It is very hard to avoid this, so let that happen and then relax your hearing and let go of the object and just listen.

Listen to sounds without hearing things. Listen to recorded music or the radio and see how images of musicians and composers, and thoughts about them, fill your mind. Let go of the imaginary musicians and composers, and let your mind rest on the sound itself.

Try the same thing with smells, tastes, and tactile sensations.

Take your time with each of these and see if you can experience different types of form without imagining them to be anything.

"Dharmas," or "phenomena," are the objects of the mental consciousness. You could investigate these by revisiting the explorations of the imaginary nature that we did before.

This time, instead of looking at the environment and the inhabitants to see what isn't there, look to see what actually is.

The Buddha used an interesting metaphor for different ways of meditating that might clarify this way of practicing. He said that if you throw a stick at a dog, the dog will chase after the stick. If you throw a stick at a lion, the lion will chase after you. Usually, we meditate like dogs, chasing after thoughts. Instead, like a lion, look right at the thinker.

Look at thoughts, mental images, and all other phenomena to see their luminous-knowing nature. They are like illusions, dreams, and mirages. When you recognize this, it is like recognizing a dream while you are still dreaming. You see that everything is made out of mind-stuff—it is merely consciousness.

NONCONCEPTUALITY AND THE UNCONDITIONED

To connect with the perfectly existent nature, let go of any idea about what it is, including the idea that everything is merely consciousness. There is really no technique or method for letting go into nonconceptuality and the unconditioned. Any technique would be artificial.

The way to practice this is to realize that whenever there is a little break in the flow of conceptuality, the perfectly existent nature is there. We cannot fabricate it and we don't need to fabricate it. Just let the experience of the perfectly existent nature come and go. Holding on to it is also a superimposition, so just let it come and go.

10
THE MIDDLE

THE BUDDHA PROPHESIED in the *Lankavatara Sutra* that four hundred years after his *parinirvana*, a monk named Naga would appear who would overcome all the extreme views of existence and nonexistence. The protector Nagarjuna fulfilled this prophecy by composing three important collections of teachings that comment on the Buddha's three turnings of the wheel of dharma.* Nagarjuna's extraordinary contribution was to recognize that the most profound view is to hold no view at all. He pointed this out through teachings on the second turning of the wheel of dharma that use logical reasoning to expose the limits of the reasoning mind. Thus he opened a "middle way" (*madhyamaka* in Sanskrit) to genuine reality that is beyond all conceptual extremes.

Nagarjuna's most important work is *The Fundamental Wisdom of the Middle Way.* It is a pivotal text in the mahayana Buddhist tradition and has been studied widely in the major Tibetan, Chinese, Japanese, and Korean schools. The main topic of this text is emptiness. In it, Nagarjuna demonstrates that everything that appears is without true nature. While it appears, it is empty. While it is empty, it appears.

---

* See Appendix 1, pages 206–7 for a description of these collections.

A key verse from *The Fundamental Wisdom* reads:

"Existence" is the view of permanence,
"Nonexistence" is the view of extinction,
Therefore, the wise do not abide
Either in existence or in nonexistence.[1]

As soon as we think, "Something is . . ." or "Something is not . . . ," that thinking obscures suchness, the way things really are. When we see a woman walking with her child and think, "She is the mother; that is her daughter," we cover over empty appearances with our concepts. When we see a new car and think, "That car was made in Japan," we cover over empty appearances with our concepts. Genuine reality is empty of "is" and "is not." It is beyond "is" and "is not." In genuine reality whatever appears is empty—right at the moment it appears. Emptiness and appearance are not two separate things. Thinking that things exist as anything other than empty appearance is mistaken.

You might wonder if there is some "middle" that is in between the extremes of existence and nonexistence that we can rest in. As the Buddha taught in the *King of Samadhi Sutra:*

"Existence" and "nonexistence" are both extremes,
"Pure" and "impure" are the same.
Therefore, abandoning all extremes,
The wise do not even abide in the middle.[2]

Here is a simple traditional demonstration that appearances are empty of the characteristics that we attribute to them:

Look at the first illustration below. You can see that the black line is short and the gray line is long. If you ask anyone, they will say the same thing. That's the way it appears to us. If I say the gray line is short, you will correct me and say that it is long.

What happens when we change things around? Look at the next illustration. In this one the gray line is short. In fact, it is the same length as the gray line in the previous illustration, but next to the long dashed line, the gray line is short. If you point to that illustration and say to someone that the gray line is long, they will tell you that it is not, that you are mistaken. We could keep going with this and make the dashed line short by putting it next to a line that was still longer, but the point is clear. Long and short do not exist in the objects themselves.

It is easy to see that long and short don't truly exist in objects. They are just labels imputed by thoughts in dependence on appearances. Things aren't truly long or short. In fact, they aren't truly anything at all! Whatever qualities you can think of—fat and thin, nice and mean, big and small, simple and complicated, light and dark, old and new, selfish and generous, beautiful and ugly, mine and yours—when we investigate, we find that they are just like long and short. They are all merely dependent imputations.

Friends turn into enemies, enemies turn into friends. That which is pleasing today is distasteful tomorrow. How can that be? It is because friend and enemy, pleasing and displeasing, do not exist in the objects themselves. Things are empty of all such characteristics.

Things are also not nonexistent. They do appear even though they have no essence. "Nonexistence" is also just imputed by thought. In a sutra called *The Pith Instructions to Katyayana,* the Buddha explains:

> Katyayana, most people in the world fixate intensely on things as being existent, and others on the thought that things are nonexistent. As a result of their clinging, they are not free from birth, aging, sickness, or death; from agony, crying, suffering, mental anguish, or agitation. Especially, they are not free in any way from the torments of death.[3]

"I exist. My body exists. My relatives and possessions exist. This world exists." These thoughts automatically bring clinging and fixation. They also bring the thoughts of nonexistence. You could lose all those things that you treasure so much. In fact, you *will* lose all those things. Therefore, clinging to existence and nonexistence is at the heart of our suffering. To free ourselves from suffering, we need to free ourselves from clinging to existence and nonexistence.

All thoughts are based on existence and nonexistence. Thinking something is "this" automatically means that it is not "that." We cling to its existence as "this" and its nonexistence as "that." If *this* is a cow, it is not a horse, a monkey, a tree, a boat, or anything other than a cow. We see it as a cow, label it as a cow, and cling to it as a cow. To free ourselves from clinging to existence and nonexistence, we need to free ourselves from all views. Nagarjuna's concluding homage from *The Fundamental Wisdom* shows that this is the main thrust of the Buddha's teachings:

Holding us in your incredible wisdom and love,
You taught us the genuine Dharma
To help us abandon all views.
I prostrate before you, Gautama.[4]

"All views" includes not only philosophical, scientific, theistic, and Buddhist views, but also all the conventional "common-sense" concepts that we unquestioningly call upon throughout our daily lives, things that seem so basic that it almost seems silly to call them "views" at all. However, it is these views that make up the vast fabric of conceptuality that binds us.

To show how pervasive and extensive our views are, Nagarjuna devotes twenty-seven chapters in *The Fundamental Wisdom* to refuting the true existence of everything we cling to, from the most sublime to the most mundane. He investigates and refutes the true existence of such basic concepts as cause and effect; coming and going; the elements; actors and actions; experiencers and experience; bondage and liberation; karmic actions and results; time; collections; mistakes; nirvana; and even views themselves. We assume that all of these things exist, but Nagarjuna analyzes them with a variety of reasonings and demonstrates that all of them are emptiness.

What would it be like to experience such emptiness? Paraphrasing the founder of the Soto Zen school in *Zen Mind, Beginner's Mind*, Suzuki Roshi describes the experience of emptiness in an evocative way: "According to Dogen-zenji, every existence is a flashing into the vast phenomenal world."[5]

REASONING

Nagarjuna's approach is rigorous and challenging. It contradicts every one of our normal assumptions, so it requires clear logical analysis to penetrate to the key point. You might wonder how logic and reasoning can cause us to realize what is beyond concepts, and how such an intellectual approach can take us beyond the intellect. Usually, we think of that as meditation's role, but in Madhyamaka, the role of reasoning is emphasized.

In the Middle Way schools, reasoning is emphasized, because it is difficult to realize the true nature of reality and attain liberation without first developing certainty in emptiness. Having an opinion that things are empty, or a general understanding of emptiness, isn't going to do much good. Emptiness does not appear to our senses and we don't ordinarily think about it either. Since it is one of the most profound and unfamiliar topics, we need many explanations and much study to come to terms with it. We already believe there are so many reasons that things exist. Each of these reasons needs to be refuted so that we can develop confidence in emptiness. Madhyamika reasoning is used to deconstruct the conventional views that bind us like insects in a spider's web.

In the Sutra tradition, practitioners train in gradually developing intellectual certainty in emptiness, and within this certainty, gradually developing direct realization through meditation. The *Lankavatara Sutra* explains the relationship of reasoning and meditation in the following verse:

> Those who study this approach with reasoning
> Will gain faith, strive in yoga, and transcend all thought.
> And those who thus rely on what does not abide
> Will find a doctrine that is like pure gold.[6]

Mipham Gyamtso expands upon the benefits of developing certainty, in the following quotation from his most important Middle Way commentary, *The Adornment of the Middle Way:*

> One must gain certainty in the unmistaken view, meditation, and practice, and abandon the false processes of dualistic thought. If one engages in this path, which estab-

lishes through valid reasoning the meaning of the Buddha's words—pure in terms of the three knowledge sources* — one will gain an extraordinary conviction in the unmistaken view, meditation, and practice. One will gain an understanding for oneself, and no one will be able to divert one from it. Seeing the great path of the Buddhas of the three times, bathed in the brilliant light of wisdom, it will be impossible not to enter it. Moreover, this conviction will come not through an external inspiration or advocacy. It will be gained not through reliance on others or the effect of some outside influence, but through the strength of one's own reasoning. This is what is meant when it is said that one will have no need of anyone else; one will be convinced on one's own account. Faith will be gained through knowledge, and thanks to this, no adversary or negative force will be able to divert one from the path.

Those who possess the eyes of such wisdom gain certainty in the unmistaken path. They have a sublime certainty that prevails over wrong views, distinguishing true from false, like well-sighted people able to distinguish forms simply by looking at them. As it was said by the Lord Maitreya:

The wise who sound with reasoning this perfect
     Dharma
Are ever guarded from the demons' hindrances;
They have a special confidence; all other views they
     vanquish—
Such are their perfect, ripened qualities that none can
     take away.[7]

_____

* The three knowledge sources are direct perception, inference, and scriptural authority.

There are differences in the way realization is developed in the Sutra tradition and in the mantra tradition, but confidence in emptiness is essential for practitioners of both. In the mantra tradition, instead of gradually developing intellectual certainty and then gradually developing direct realization through meditation, practitioners are directly introduced to genuine reality through extraordinary methods such as the empowerments and the practices of the development stage and the completion stage. The experience of genuine reality is the same for both types of practitioner, but the methods are different. Nevertheless, while powerful vajrayana methods produce glimpses of realization, without certainty in emptiness it is extremely difficult to sustain this, and in postmeditation it is difficult to have sacred outlook. Without gaining confidence in emptiness, it is easy for mantrayana practitioners to lapse into ordinariness between practice sessions.

EMPTINESS AND MIND ONLY

Before we look into the details of the Middle Way reasonings, we should note that abandoning all views has important implications for the Mind Only approach that we discussed previously. In the Mind Only system, practitioners cut through beliefs in the existence of outer objects, and in the duality of perceivers and what is perceived, by recognizing that all phenomena are only mind. However, this might leave a belief that consciousness itself truly exists as some type of substance. Because of this tendency, Chittamatrins are sometimes referred to as "proponents of consciousness."

Taking consciousness as real is a stain that prevents us from fully realizing the dynamic display of appearance-emptiness. This is a subtle point, but one that some Madhyamikas, such as Chandrakirti, refute at length. The problem with believing that consciousness truly exists is that we then take it to be a substantial basis for phenomena and cling to it as a self. Since much of our belief in the self is connected to clinging to "my mind," it is important to recognize that mind, too, is empty.

Once again, we have a quotation from Mipham Gyamtso that we can use in order to contemplate this important point. This is from his commentary on Maitreya's *Distinguishing Phenomena and Pure Being*:

> A slight remnant of a subtle hypothetical tenet persists within the Chittamatra system in the sense that true existence is posited for the essence of the ineffable consciousness. If one demonstrates the flaws in this supposition through logical reasoning and asserts that this consciousness itself, which is free of perceived and perceiver, is also devoid of true existence, such that mind itself is a union of this emptiness and primordially pure clear light, this is authentic Madhyamaka.
>
> A distinction can, therefore, be made between these two Mahayana schools, Chittamatra and Madhyamaka, with respect to the crucial point of whether this subtle assumption has been cut through or not, but the meditative and post-meditative phases as practiced in both are so nearly identical that even the great pandits and mahasiddhas of the noble land [India] with good reason made no distinction between the two as far as the actual practice of Mahayana is concerned.[8]

ANOTHER INTERLUDE

AND NOW FOR SOMETHING completely different . . .

THE DINOSAUR SKETCH FROM
Monty Python's Flying Circus[1]

Television Host [Graham Chapman]: Good evening. Tonight—
dinosaurs. I have here sitting in the studio next to me an elk.
Aaagghhhh! Oh, I'm sorry, Anne Elk, Mrs. Anne Elk.

Miss Elk [John Cleese]: Miss.

Host: Miss Anne Elk, who is an expert on the . . .

Elk: No, no, no, Anne Elk.

Host: What?

Elk: Anne Elk, not Anne Expert.

Host: No, no, I was saying that you, Miss Elk, were an, A.N. not
A.N.N.E., expert . . .

Elk: Oh!

Host: . . . on elks—I'm sorry, on dinosaurs.

Elk: Yes, I certainly am, Chris, how very true, my word yes!

Host: Now, Miss Elk—Anne—you have a new theory about the
brontosaurus.

Elk: Could I just say, Chris, for one moment that I have a new
theory about the brontosaurus?

Host: Er . . . exactly. What is it?

Elk: Where?

Host: No, no, no. What is your theory?

Elk: Oh, what is my theory?

Host: Yes.

Elk: Oh what is my theory, that it is. Yes, well you may well ask, what is my theory.

Host: I am asking.

Elk: And well you may. Yes my word you may well ask what it is, this theory of mine. Well, this theory that I have—that is to say, which is mine—. . . is mine.

Host: I know it's yours. What is it?

Elk: Where? Oh, what is my theory?

Host: Yes!

Elk: Oh, my theory that I have follows the lines I am about to relate. Ahem. Ahem. Ahem. Ahem. Ahem. Ahem.

Host: Oh God.

Elk: Ahem. Ahem. Ahem. Ahem. Ahem. Ahem. Ahem. Ahem. Ahem. Ahem. Ahem. Ahem. The Theory, by A. Elk. That's A for Anne, it's not by a elk.

Host: Right. . . .

Elk: This theory which belongs to me is as follows. Ahem. Ahem. This is how it goes. Ahem. The next thing that I am about to say is my theory. Ahem. Ready?

The Theory by A. Elk brackets Miss brackets. My theory is along the following lines.

Host: Oh God.

Elk: All brontosauruses are thin at one end, much MUCH thicker in the middle, and then thin again at the far end. That is the theory that I have and which is mine, and what it is too.

Host: That's it, is it?

Elk: Right, Chris.

Host: Well, Anne, this theory of yours seems to have hit the nail on the head.

Elk: And it's mine.

Host: Thank you for coming along to the studio.

Elk: My pleasure, Chris.

Host: Er . . . Britain's newest wasp farm . . .

Elk: It's been a lot of fun.

Host: . . . opened last week . . .

Elk: Saying what my theory is.

Host: Yes, thank you.

Elk: And whose it is.

Host: Yes. . . . opened last week . . .

Elk: I have another theory.

Host: Not today, thank you.

Elk: My theory number two, which is the second theory that I have. Ahem! This theory . . .

Host: Oh look . . . shut up!

Elk: . . . is what I am about to say . . .

Host: Oh please shut up!

Elk: . . . which, with what I have said, are the two theories that are mine and belong to me.

Host: Look, if you don't shut up I shall shoot you.

Elk: Ahem! My brace of theories, which I possess the ownership of, which belongs to me . . .

BANG

That's one way to abandon all views.

11

SVATANTRIKAS AND PRASANGIKAS

INTERESTINGLY, WHILE THE heart of the Middle Way teachings is abandoning all views, there seem to be an awful lot of views about classifying the Middle Way teachings. Scholars argue about schools, subschools, and sub-subschools; about which teachers and teachings fit where, what are the correct bases for classification, the historical realities, and on and on. There are lots of disagreements about which schools are right and which are wrong, which are the best and which are the worst, which are good and which are bad. Frankly, all these conflicts seem to obscure a lot more than they clarify, while preventing people from seeing the valuable and complementary contributions of the different approaches. I think the most helpful way to look at the Middle Way schools is to see how they emphasize different aspects of practice and different stages of realization.

A related issue is the temptation for students of Madhyamaka to think, "I am a Prasangika," or "I am a Shentongpa," or whatever. The problem with this is that when we think "I," we take the self to truly exist, and when we think, "Prasangika" we take phenomena to truly exist. Since all Madhyamikas refute the true existence of both the self and phenomena, at that moment we are not Madhyamikas at all!

The most basic division between Middle Way schools is between those who emphasize the empty aspect of genuine reality and those who emphasize the luminous or wisdom aspect. Since genuine reality is beyond all concepts of what it is, or is not, neither description is really adequate. To help us gradually develop direct nonconceptual experience, first the empty aspect is presented. After we develop confidence in emptiness, wisdom is pointed out. If wisdom is presented first, it is easy to mistake wisdom for a thing or a self. If only emptiness is presented, we can become fixated on a nihilistic concept of emptiness. That is why the presentation needs to be done in stages. In India, those who emphasized the empty aspect were referred to as "proponents of absence of nature." Those who emphasized the luminous or wisdom aspect were referred to as "Yogachara-Madhyamikas."

Later scholars called the schools that emphasize the empty aspect Rangtong Madhyamaka, which means "self-empty Middle Way," because they teach that phenomena are empty of an essence, or self-empty. The school that emphasizes the luminosity or wisdom aspect of genuine reality became known as Shentong Madhyamaka, which means the "empty-of-other Middle Way," because they point out that genuine reality is empty of what is other—defilements—but not empty of wisdom.

We will begin with Rangtong Madhyamaka, and look at Shentong Madhyamaka in a later chapter.

THREE STAGES OF ANALYSIS

Rangtong Madhyamaka is subdivided into two subschools: the Svatantrika, or Autonomy school, and the Prasangika, or Consequence school. All these divisions may seem confusing and aca-

demic, but since they represent progressively more subtle under-
standings of genuine reality, it is a helpful framework. Our own
understanding and experience tends to unfold in these stages, so
recognizing these patterns helps us to know how to progress on
the path.

A good framework for understanding the classifications of
Rangtong is what Madhyamikas call "the three stages of analysis." These are stages of investigation into the nature of phenomena. The first stage is the stage of *no analysis*. This is the way
things appear to ordinary people who have not begun to analyze
the nature of phenomena. At this stage you imagine that things
exist in just the way they appear; the self, objects, the world, the
past, and the future—all appear to exist, and they are described
as though they exist.

Once you begin to analyze the nature of phenomena using
Madhyamaka reasonings, you discover that you can't find anything that truly exists at all. Things appear, but you can't find any
nature to them. You understand that they *do not* exist. This is
called the stage of *slight analysis*. This is the stage emphasized in
the Heart Sutra:

> . . . there is no form, no feeling, no perception, no forma-
> tion, no consciousness; no eye, no ear, no nose, no tongue,
> no body, no mind; no appearance, no sound, no smell, no
> taste, no touch, no dharmas; no eye dhatu up to no mind
> dhatu, no dhatu of dharmas, no mind consciousness
> dhatu; no ignorance, no end of ignorance up to no old age
> and death, no end of old age and death; no suffering, no
> origin of suffering, no cessation of suffering, no path, no
> wisdom, no attainment, and no nonattainment.[1]

Why is this called the stage of slight analysis? Because nonexistence is still a concept. Nonexistence and existence depend

upon each other. Without the idea of existence, there can be no idea of nonexistence. The emptiness that is understood at the stage of slight analysis is the "approximate ultimate." It is similar to genuine reality, but it is not the authentic genuine reality. It is a mental image of emptiness, not the real emptiness that is beyond concept or description. The *slight* in "slight analysis" makes it sound unimportant, but gaining an intellectual understanding of emptiness is extremely important. It is only when it is compared with direct realization that this stage seems slight.

The stage of *thorough analysis* is the stage where all concepts about existence and nonexistence have been pacified and genuine reality is seen just as it is, free from any conceptual fabrications whatsoever. This is the "actual ultimate," which can never be expressed in words. Nagarjuna explains in *The Fundamental Wisdom of the Middle Way* that the reality of the stage of thorough analysis is:

Unknowable by analogy; peace;
Not of the fabric of fabrications;
Nonconceptual; free of distinctions—
These are the characteristics of the precise nature.[2]

Shantideva also explains this in *The Way of the Bodhisattva*:

The absolute is not within the reach of intellect,
For intellect is grounded in the relative.[3]

Because only exceptional practitioners are able to immediately click into the actual ultimate, most of us need to progress gradually through the three stages of analysis. The main distinction between the Autonomy school and the Consequence school is that the Autonomy school presents a gradual path, which emphasizes the stage of slight analysis: the nonexistence of phenomena, or the approximate ultimate. The Consequence school presents the sudden path, which emphasizes the stage of thorough analysis, which is beyond concepts.

This is extensively explained in Mipham Gyamtso's commentary on Shanta-rakshita's *Madhyamakalankara, The Adornment of the Middle Way*. In this commentary Mipham Rinpoche shows how Shanta-rakshita synthesized the views of the entire mahayana by bringing together the streams of Chittamatra and Madhyamaka. He also shows how clarifying the distinction between the approximate ultimate and the actual ultimate is a key point in understanding the Middle Way teachings. Mipham Rinpoche writes:

> If it is not pointed out right at the beginning that phenomena have no true existence, there is no means of dispelling our mistaken clinging to reality. For we have grown accustomed to it from unoriginated time. Nevertheless, if this alone is taught as the ultimate truth, certain persons of weak understanding might think that "nonexistence" is the ultimate reality. . . . And clinging to such "emptiness," such people become incurable. This manner of clinging can be of two kinds. One can cling to emptiness as a positive value, a thing (*dngos po*), and one can cling to it as a nonthing, a mere absence (*dngos med*). One may say here that it is improper to cling to any conceptual extreme. But if definite knowledge [of the approximate ultimate], which is elicited by rational investigation and is the nectar-spring of profound emptiness, is spurned in the belief that there should be no mental activity of any kind, one falls into a thick and murky state devoid of thought. This renders it very difficult to perceive this profound reality, to realize it, and to bring it into experience. . . .

Consequently, it is simply through the approximate ultimate that clinging to reality is, as a first step, destroyed. Later, by means of the teaching on the actual ultimate, clinging to nonreality is also halted. . . . This demonstrates the need for the approximate ultimate.[4]

DIFFERENT APPROACHES
TO APPARENT REALITY

Svatantrikas and Prasangikas do not disagree about the actual ultimate: both agree that genuine reality is beyond all fabrications. The main difference between Svatantrikas and Prasangikas is that Svatantrikas assert the approximate ultimate. In addition, there are interesting differences in the way these schools describe apparent reality.

Svatantrikas describe apparent reality in different ways: Some follow the presentation of the Sutra school and say that apparent reality is made of partless particles and moments of consciousness. Others follow the presentation of the Mind Only school and say that apparent reality is best described as mind alone. (This is similar to the way quantum physicists describe light: sometimes they describe it as particles, and sometimes they describe it as waves. Is light made of particles or of waves? Well, its actual nature is beyond being made of particles or waves. Those are only concepts we use to describe it.)

Prasangikas do not accept any philosophical presentation of apparent reality. They say that apparent reality can only be posited from the perspective of no analysis. The reason for this is that as soon as you begin to analyze apparent phenomena, you do not find anything at all. The only way to describe apparent reality is from the perspective of worldly people. Worldly people look at appearances and see them arising due to causes and conditions, and that's all apparent reality is—nothing more.

Jamgön Kongtrul Lodrö Thayé explains the schools' different approaches to conventional reality very clearly in *The Treasury of Knowledge*:

[Svatantrikas and Prasangikas] do disagree, however, about the presentation of conventional reality. Svatantrikas think that this should not be done according to the conventions of worldly people, because that would involve the possibility of error, as worldly people use conventions in a casual way without any rational analysis. Instead, they posit conventional reality in keeping with those who know how to apply reasonings, such as Proponents of Cognition (Vijnaptivadins) or Sautrantikas. They maintain that even though Proponents of Cognition and the others have deviated from a correct understanding of ultimate reality, they have not done so with conventional reality. . . .

Prasangika masters . . . think that conventional reality should be posited according to the conventions of worldly people, not according to the proponents of other philosophical systems. This is because, in the same way that noble beings are the only valid authorities (*pramana, tshad ma*) for ultimate reality, worldly people are the only valid authorities for the positing of conventional reality.[5]

THE ORIGIN OF THE NAMES
SVATANTRIKA AND PRASANGIKA

The names Svatantrika and Prasangika were not used in the Indian Madhyamaka tradition, but were invented by Tibetan scholars when classifying the teachings of the Indian tradition. The names themselves refer to the methods each school uses to debate and clarify the view. Svatantrikas make assertions about emptiness (these assertions are the approximate ultimate) and present logical reasoning to demonstrate their case. These reasonings are said to exist autonomously (*svatantra*). Prasangikas, emphasizing the genuine ultimate, make no assertions of their own, but use logical reasoning to demonstrate the illogical consequences (*prasanga*) of other people's views. Jamgön Kongtrul explains the Prasangika method in *The Treasury of Knowledge* in the following terms:

> A thesis, whatever it may be, is the creation of the intellect, and the intellect is a conventional, mistaken cognition. Therefore, for Prasangikas, there are no independently verifiable [autonomous] theses or assertions. Even nonarising, freedom from elaborations, and so forth are not put forth as independently verifiable theses for the following two reasons. (1) Although phenomena, persons, and so forth (which are verbally stated) have never existed, non-Buddhist and Buddhist Realists fixate upon them as real entities, because they have fallen into the extremes of superimposition or denial. Reasonings that demonstrate nonarising and so forth are stated only to banish such unwarranted reification. (2) Once that reification is overturned, the intellect that clings to nonentities also must be renounced; and thus it is taught that the ultimate is beyond the intellect and without any clinging.[6]

To get a deeper feeling for the approaches of these two schools, it would be good to contemplate Jamgön Kongtrul's summary of their views in *The Treasury of Knowledge*:

> Appearances exist relatively, they are like illusions.
> In genuine actuality, nothing exists—it is like space.
> This is the position of the Autonomy school.[7]

And:

Apparent reality is whatever mind imagines, it is asserted
  following worldly tradition.
Genuine reality is beyond fabrications—inexpressible
  and inconceivable.
This is the Consequence school's tradition.[8]

12

GREAT REASONINGS
OF THE MIDDLE WAY

MADHYAMIKAS USE FIVE main methods to show the internal contradictions in realist views that things truly exist. Since these methods are powerful contemplations to undermine our materialistic attachments, we will go into them in some detail. But first the headlines . . .

The five reasonings are as follows:

- *The analysis of a nature* shows that phenomena are neither one thing nor many things, therefore phenomena do not truly exist.
- *The analysis of causes*, or *the vajra sliver reasoning*, shows that phenomena do not arise from themselves; phenomena do not arise from something other than themselves; phenomena do not arise from both of these; and phenomena do not arise without causes. Therefore, phenomena do not arise and they do not truly exist.
- *The analysis of results* shows that phenomena that are existing results do not arise, and phenomena that are nonexisting results do not arise, and therefore phenomena do not truly exist.

- *The analysis of both causes and results* shows that one cause does not produce one result; one cause does not produce many results; many causes do not produce one result; and many causes do not produce many results. Therefore, phenomena do not truly exist.

- *The analysis of interdependence* shows that there are no phenomena that exist under their own power; they only appear through the gathering of causes and conditions. Therefore phenomena do not truly exist.

You can see that these reasonings have a similar structure. They basically argue that *if things truly existed the way we conceive them to exist, then logically they would have to exist/arise/result in certain ways, and since this is not the case, they do not exist as we conceive.* Since things do not truly exist, the nature of phenomena is emptiness.

Although it is often said that these reasonings "prove" things are empty, or "prove" that phenomena have no nature, this is not quite the case. What each of the reasonings proves is that our normal beliefs about existence are illogical. This opens a space for us to see the genuine nature of phenomena.

We will look at each of these reasonings in detail, but since they can be difficult to contemplate, I would like to make a few preliminary suggestions. Don't just read through the arguments once or twice. Contemplate each of the reasonings repeatedly, one at a time, over the course of a couple of weeks. Because our habit of believing that phenomena truly exist is deeply ingrained and we reinforce it all day long, it is not easy to glimpse a different reality. When you do, you can be sure that your habitual way of seeing will quickly cover it over, so don't try to cling to these experiences. Instead, contemplate the reasonings again and again.

Begin each contemplation session by patiently reviewing the reasoning to make sure you understand the logic. They are not complicated, but they are unusual ways of looking at things. If you don't understand what the point of the exercise is, it is easy to get frustrated by the arguments and turn off to the contemplation. If you find you are turning off, it sometimes helps to remember that people have contemplated these reasonings for almost two thousand years for the very reason that they actually work: they have the power to transform our understanding and experience.

Once you have understood the logic of the reasoning, slowly contemplate the illustrating images. The images really help make the issues tangible. It is also very helpful to try to come up with examples and images of your own.

Once I was going on solitary retreat, both to meditate and to study Chandrakirti's *Entering the Middle Way*. Since several of Chandrakirti's examples involve seeds and shoots, I went out and bought some sunflower seeds at my local hardware store to grow during the retreat. I thought it might make the examples more vivid. I got a small flowerpot, planted about a dozen seeds, and put them on the table where I ate my meals. Since I am a New Yorker at heart, and never developed an interest in gardening, I was a bit clueless about how to proceed. I watered my little garden every day, but to my disappointment, not a damn thing happened. Finally, after about ten days, I sat down for breakfast and saw a couple of little shoots in the pot. I was surprised and delighted. I vividly saw what Chandrakirti was talking about. After the retreat, I was having dinner with a friend who is an avid gardener, and I asked her why my project produced such meager results. She said I had probably watered the seeds too much. After that I stopped watering the seeds for a few days and about eight more shoots came up. Unfortunately, this story has an unhappy ending. I transplanted the shoots to the backyard, expecting to get a bunch of big sunflowers by the end of the summer. When I went out to check on their progress the next day, they had all been eaten by insects. My plants were not just empty—they were nonexistent!

When you are having difficulty with a contemplation, it sometimes helps to ask yourself what you are imagining that contradicts the logic of the reasoning. By doing this, you might see what you superimpose on phenomena that makes you believe they are not empty. For example, if you go into the kitchen and see dirty dishes in the sink, and you think that your friend or spouse caused the dirty dishes, ask yourself if the dirty dishes you perceive actually arose from that cause, or is that friend or spouse just a projection? This is not a question about being right or wrong about the cause of something, but simply of recognizing the true nature of what is appearing.

Finally, as with any contemplation, you need to find a balance between diligently contemplating the investigation and simply letting go and resting the mind. From time to time these reasonings can tie you in knots and get quite frustrating. That is par for the course.

THE ANALYSIS OF A NATURE

It is important to consider what it means to think that things *do* truly exist. If we aren't clear about that, it will be hard to understand the reasonings that demonstrate their lack of true existence. Normally, when we say that things exist, we mean that they exist, as Madhyamikas say, "from their own side," with their own characteristics. They are substantial. This desk was made somewhere, at some time, out of certain materials, and now it is here. It is my desk. It is really here; it is not just a projection of a desk, or a mere appearance, like a desk in a dream. When I leave the room, it will still be here, and unless someone moves it, anyone who comes into the room will see the same desk that I see. This is the way we think things exist and what the Madhyamaka reasonings ask us to reconsider.

The first reasoning asks, "If things truly exist, do they exist as one thing or many things?" Using this analysis we investigate to see if things have a nature or an essence. We should contemplate this. The reasoning is very simple. Here is how it might be formally presented:

All phenomena, such as this desk, do not truly exist, because they are neither one thing nor many things, just like a desk in a dream.

This desk is merely an appearance. It is not a single unit, because it has parts: It has a front and a back, a top and a bottom. When you look at it from one side, the other side does not appear. It has drawers. It has a work surface. It has legs. This desk is also not many units, because each of the parts can be divided into smaller units, ad infinitum. There are no single units that are the basic building blocks for the larger units.* The desk is neither one thing nor many things. If something truly exists, it would have to exist as one thing or many things since these two are mutually exclusive. Therefore, "desk" is just a concept imputed on mere appearance. It has no nature or essence of its own.

Let's try that again:

All phenomena, such as a beach, do not truly exist, because they are neither one thing nor many things, just like a reflection of a beach in a mirror.

---

* In chapter 7, pages 69–71, we saw how the existence of partless particles and irreducible moments of consciousness proposed by the Vaibhashikas and Sautrantikas is refuted, and that the same reasoning applies to the particles proposed by Western science.

It is easy to see that a beach is not a single unit, because it is made up of a vast number of grains of sand—take away all the grains of sand and you won't find any beach anywhere, nor will you find the beach in each grain of sand. Do the grains of sand exist as single units? No, they are each made of molecules, which are made of atoms, which are made of protons, electrons, and neutrons, which are made of quarks, which are made of string, which have parts because they are extended objects. Since there are no single units to serve as building blocks, a beach is not many things either. Therefore, a beach, and all other things that are collections, are only appearances and do not exist from their own side.

These are examples of analyzing objects that seem to be substantial, because they extend in space. We can apply the same analysis to things that extend in time:

All phenomena, such as a piece of music, do not truly exist, because they are neither one thing nor many things, just like an echo in an empty valley.

A song, or a piece of music, is not one thing, because it is made of many notes or sounds. When you listen to music, there is the part of the piece that has already been played, the part of the piece that has not yet been played, and the part of the piece you are actually hearing at the moment. That moment of sound is also not a single unit, because it has a beginning, a middle, and an end. You can't hear the whole piece of music in one moment, so it is not a single unit and you can't find any basic units that the music is made of either. Therefore a piece of music does not truly exist.

Here is a nice quote from Aryadeva that shows how moments do not truly exist:

See how an instant has an end,
And likewise a beginning and a middle.
Because an instant is in turn three instants,
Momentariness is not the nature of the world.[1]

Perhaps the most interesting and practical thing to analyze is friends and enemies, because so much of our happiness and suffering comes from believing that friends and enemies truly exist:

All phenomena, such as friends and enemies, do not truly exist, because they are neither one thing nor many things, just like friends and enemies in a movie.

Friends and enemies are not single units, because they appear in so many different ways and they are always changing. No one is always nice or always nasty. Friends and enemies are sometimes sleepy, feisty, loud, quiet, or boring. Sometimes they are angry and sometimes they are happy. Sometimes you hear their voices on the telephone, read their messages on e-mail, or meet them face-to-face. Sometimes friends turn into enemies and enemies turn into friends. It is fairly easy to see that friends and enemies do not exist as single units. You can analyze them and see that they are not made of particles, and you can analyze them to show that there are no single instants of their existence. Therefore friends and enemies are just appearances, like friends and enemies in a movie.

Finally, the most important and personal thing we can analyze is suffering itself:

All phenomena, such as suffering, do not truly exist, because they are neither one thing nor many things, just like suffering in a dream.

The analysis of a nature is the simplest reasoning to understand. Jamgön Kongtrul makes the point in his summary of the analysis of a nature in *The Treasury of Knowledge* that it is also the root of all the other reasonings:

Reasons stating that a sprout and other things are devoid of both real unity and real plurality prove that such things have no reality. This reasoning that something is neither a single unit nor a plurality is the root of all reasonings that negate true existence, which all four Buddhist philosophical systems consider to be the object of negation.[2]

13

NO ARISING

WHENEVER SOMETHING APPEARS, we assume it exists. To say that it exists means that the appearance is based on an "object." If an object exists, there must also be a history of the production, or arising, of that object. We assume that the object "arose," or "came into existence," "appeared," or "resulted" from a cause or a source. We see our lunch on a plate in front of us and think that it was prepared by someone in the kitchen. If we were to think about it any further, perhaps while we're waiting for our lunch companion to return from making a phone call, we might say that the grains were grown on a farm and processed in certain ways, the vegetables were grown in different regions and shipped to the local market, the meat (if we eat meat) came from a certain kind of animal, and so on.

The idea of production, or arising, goes hand in hand with the idea of true existence. If something truly exists, it must have been produced. If it was produced, it must exist. On the other hand, things that don't really exist, such as things seen in dreams, are not produced. The dream car was not produced in a factory.

You might disagree and say that the dream car was produced—it was produced by the mind. This brings out a key point in the Middle Way teachings. Appearances, like cars in dreams, are not refuted. The mere appearance of dependent arising is not refuted. What is refuted is any basis for the appearances: truly existing objects, their histories, and the like. This includes refuting substantially existing mind, if we imagine such a thing. The distinction between dependently arisen mere appearances and the production of truly existent things is subtle. Understanding it requires a lot of analysis and reflection.

The second Madhyamaka reasoning, the analysis of causes, asks us to examine production, or arising, to see if it can truly be found. It is a way to get at our assumptions that there are objects, and that these objects have real histories. The reasoning goes like this: if things truly exist, then they would have to be produced, or arise, and the production or arising must be from one or the other of the following:

- from themselves
- from something other than themselves
- from both of these
- without a cause

These four alternatives are all there could be—there is no fifth possibility.

We don't usually question the arising of things. When we do begin to think about arising, sometimes it looks like we assume that things arise or appear from themselves; for example, "When I go home at night, my house appears, because it is there," or, "If I go to Los Angeles, I can see Hollywood." We are assuming that we see things because they already exist: the objects are out there, and they arise or manifest from themselves.

Sometimes we assume that things arise from something other than themselves; for example, "This computer was produced in a factory," or, "These plants grew from seeds." In these cases we are assuming that the things originally did not exist, but were produced from other things.

Sometimes we assume that things arise from some combination of these two; for example, "This hamburger was made in the kitchen from hamburger meat." Here the assumption is that something arose from itself with the aid of other causes and conditions.

Sometimes we think that things arise without cause; for example, "It was a random accident," or "The thought just popped into my head."

There are lots of scientific and philosophical arguments that are developed to back up the different instinctive explanations, but from an ordinary point of view, we take arising for granted. We have implicit assumptions about the way things arise and we always have explanations, whether they are philosophically or scientifically consistent or not. You might feel that arising does not have to be logically justified at all since it is an observable fact, but that is not the case. Arising is a concept that we superimpose on direct experience. It is not something we directly perceive.

The analysis of causes helps bring to the surface hidden assumptions and misconceptions that cover over phenomena's true nature—emptiness. By recognizing the true nature of phenomena we understand their equality and free ourselves from grasping and clinging to them as real. That is why this investigation is so important.

Thrangu Rinpoche introduces this reasoning in *The Open Door to Emptiness* in the following way:

> Emptiness is not an easy idea to grasp at first. Because it is not so easy, we will approach the notion of emptiness from the standpoint of how, if at all, results arise from causes in order to see that, while phenomena certainly function according to a successive pattern, one condition arising out of another, nonetheless the actual arising itself can never

be discovered, in other words, in the ultimate sense there is no reality to arising. By a careful analysis we can gain an intellectual appreciation of emptiness.[1]

This analysis is difficult and counterintuitive. It doesn't do much good to rush through the contemplations. In fact, they should probably come with a warning label, something like:

CAUTION: Keep this investigation out of reach of children. Use only as directed. Contemplate for short periods and repeat frequently (except as advised by a physician). These contemplations may cause irritability, nausea, or drowsiness. When doing these contemplations, caution should be exercised in operating machinery or motor vehicles.

The analysis of causes was presented briefly by Nagarjuna in *The Fundamental Wisdom of the Middle Way*. Later, Chandrakirti made it the central investigation in his general commentary, which is called the *Madhyamakavatara*, or *Entering the Middle Way*. Nagarjuna begins his presentation of the analysis of causes with the following verse:

Not from self, not from other,
Not from both, nor without cause:
Things do not arise
At any place, at any time.[2]

Chandrakirti investigates this topic using Prasangika, or Consequentialist, methods. He does not make assertions of his own, but uses logical reasoning to demonstrate the illogical consequences of other people's views. We will look at the analysis of causes following his approach.

Arising from Self

Generally, we feel that objects exist and that by looking at them we see them. If we sit in a restaurant waiting for a friend, we assume the friend exists and hope that he is on his way to join us. If he is late, we wonder if something happened to him. When he walks in the door, we think he arrived from somewhere else: he manifested. In essence, our friend seemed to manifest from himself. We don't think he appeared out of thin air, nor do we think of him as having been produced by some other agency. He appeared from himself. He arose from himself. Of course, we don't consciously think about arising in this way. We take it for granted. In fact, making appointments and expecting people to show up works pretty well in the world. It is useful. (That is why Prasangikas don't abandon worldly conventions.)

When you begin to analyze "arising from self," however, you start to see serious shortcomings with this explanation. Most basically, if something already exists, why does it need to arise again? To say that it arose is meaningless, because it already exists! This is one reason that it doesn't make sense to say that things arise from themselves.

Also, if things really did arise from themselves, they would arise endlessly, because their causes would always be present. If our friend arose from himself, he should always be present.

If things give rise to themselves, then causes produce results that are the same as themselves. But this is not what we observe — cause and result are not the same thing.

If we try to salvage the explanation that things arise from themselves, saying that our friend was unmanifest before he got to the restaurant and then manifested when he walked in the door, then it would logically follow that an unmanifest friend and a manifest friend are the same!

Do friends, houses, and cities really arise from themselves? Through repeatedly contemplating this question, we can remove the misconception that things arise from themselves.

ARISING FROM OTHER

One down, three to go. We need to investigate the next logical possibility: that things could arise from something other than themselves. In the context of investigating true existence, "other" means that two things are truly different. They are distinct entities. This is a key point to bear in mind as we go through this investigation.

Take a look at a drinking glass. A little research on the Internet shows that the process of glassmaking begins with sand, soda ash, limestone, and other raw materials. These are melted together in a furnace at very high temperatures. The molten glass is formed in a machine or blown into a mold to produce the final shape. The shaped glass goes through various stages of heat treatment, coating, and cooling. The finished product is packaged and shipped, and eventually arrives in your kitchen.

It certainly seems that a glass is truly different from the sand, soda ash, and limestone that went into the furnace. Surely, this must be a case of arising from other. Here is a contemplation to investigate this:

Look at a glass in front of you. Did the glass and its ingredients ever exist as "other"—as completely separate entities? If they did, then why couldn't the glass arise from peanut butter, jelly, and bread? If the glass arose from causes that were different from itself, it would have the same relationship to its causes and noncauses alike. Everything would be "other"—as much as the peanut butter, jelly, and bread were other, the sand, soda ash, and limestone would be the same. If things did truly exist as distinct entities, and they did arise from something other than themselves, then anything could arise from anything, because they are all equally "other." Things that are causes and things that are not causes would be equally distinct from things that are results.

Chandrakirti illustrates this absurd consequence of the belief that things arise from other with a lovely image. He says that if this really were the case, then darkness could arise from a fire's flame.

Furthermore, if one thing causes another thing to arise, the cause must come first and be succeeded by the thing produced. Otherwise it is not a cause. Causes cease as their results are produced. The sand, soda ash, and limestone are consumed in the furnace as the molten glass appears. If causes continued, they would produce results endlessly, but that is not what we observe. A cause cannot produce a result if the two exist at the same time, because the result would already exist, so how could the cause be considered the cause of it?

If a cause truly exists, it would be distinct from, independent from, unconnected with the result, so how could it bring about the result? Also, since the cause ceases as the result arises, they do not exist at the same time. Without being simultaneously present, how can causes and results be said to be either the same or different from each other?

Nevertheless, in the normal mode of the waking state, things do appear to arise in a consistent way. If we put wood in the furnace instead of sand, we will not produce glass. You might think that this is because the things that are causes have a potential to produce certain results and not others, but since the cause ceases as the result appears, any potential in the cause would cease with it. And it cannot be said that the cause's potential transfers to the result, because for that to happen, they would have to exist simultaneously; but as we have seen, it is impossible for cause and result to exist simultaneously.

You might think that the cause has the power to produce the result because they are in the same continuum, but as we discussed previously, continua are just imputed by thought and have no true existence. They are like the water in a river that looks the same but constantly changes.

These are difficult points to penetrate since "arising from other" seems so natural to us, but this is not just word games. Go slowly and you will get it. In order to pursue this investigation, it helps to think of examples of your own.

At this point it is probably good to recall that we are not refuting the arising of appearances in predictable, consistent ways. We are investigating whether there is any basis or nature to these appearances. Although events do seem to occur consistently, we are asking if there is any ultimate reality to them. The glass appears vividly right now, but has no truly existent nature and no truly existent past. Any production or arising we can think of is just a concept superimposed on this vivid appearance. When you look at the glass in front of you, you cannot find its arising.

Through repeatedly contemplating in this way, we can overcome the illusion that things arise from other.

ARISING FROM BOTH SELF AND OTHER

Since the arising of things really does seem to occur, it is tempting to think that self-arising and other-arising together might cure the logical flaws that each of them possess separately. In fact, all the logical flaws of the two individual views are still present when you combine them, and so arising from self and other together is also impossible. Chandrakirti dispatches this explanation with the following analogy: since one sesame seed can produce sesame oil, many sesame seeds can produce a lot of oil; but since one grain of sand cannot produce any sesame oil, many grains of sand cannot produce any sesame oil, either.

ARISING WITHOUT CAUSE

When you analyze causeless arising, it is easy to see absurd consequences. If things arose causelessly, then everything would always be present, or else nothing would ever be present. This is because causes and noncauses would be equally capable or incapable of producing results. The fact that things arise sometimes, and at other times do not, shows that things arise when their causes and conditions gather. They do not arise causelessly.

On a very practical level, if things arose without cause, we can see there would be no reason for people to go to the trouble of growing and preparing food, building houses, making a living, or all of the many other things we do. Why bother, since food, buildings, and income would produce themselves?

THE PUNCH LINE

In this way, we can analyze arising from self, from other, from both of these together, and from neither of these (that is, without causes) to show that "arising" cannot be found. When we gain confidence that there is no arising, we will understand that there are no truly existent things. This does not refute the mere appearance of arising, like the arising that takes place in dreams or movies. It shows that the nature of all these appearances is emptiness.

Chandrakirti states this conclusion in the following two lines:

Since things do not arise from self, other, both, nor without cause,
They have no inherent nature at all.[3]

Chandrakirti arrived at this conclusion through a process of
logical investigation, but this same point was realized by
Milarepa directly through meditation, as we can see from his
song "No Birth, No Base, and Union":

What defines appearances is that they've never been born
If birth seems to happen it's just clinging, nothing more.
What defines samsara is its lack of a base or a root,
If there is a base or root, that's only a thought.[4]

14

FURTHER REASONINGS

THE FIRST MADHYAMAKA reasoning, the analysis of a nature, demonstrates that since all phenomena are beyond being one thing or many things, they have no essence. The second reasoning, the analysis of causes, demonstrates that since phenomena cannot arise from any of the four possibilities, they do not truly exist. The third reasoning, the analysis of results, is similar to the analysis of causes, but comes at it from a different angle. It again investigates our assumptions about causality, but instead of looking at the origin of phenomena, as we did in the analysis of cause, the analysis of results looks more directly at the appearing phenomena themselves.

THE ANALYSIS OF RESULTS

The analysis of results says: if things truly exist, then they must either exist at the time of their causes or not exist at the time of their causes (or both, or neither). This may seem like an odd formulation, but investigating in this way is a very direct method of stripping away concepts of substantiality. It provides a clear, logical framework for analyzing the true existence of causes and results.

One way to begin this investigation is to produce something.

Make a sound by snapping your fingers, clapping your hands, or tapping on something, and examine that resulting sound. If the vividly appearing sound truly exists, then before you produced it, it must have been existing, not existing, both, or neither. If it is none of these, the sound is merely an appearance with no base or root.

If the sound already existed, how did snapping your fingers produce it?

If the sound did not already exist, how did snapping your fingers produce it?

As we have seen previously, when two things exist at the same time, one cannot produce the other, because the other already exists: it needs no further production. When two things do not exist at the same time, one cannot produce the other, because it cannot act upon something that is nonexistent. Another reason that an existing thing cannot produce a nonexisting thing is that phenomena are momentary; therefore, the first one will cease before the second one arises.

To get around this problem, you might think that perhaps the cause exists first and continues to exist as the result is produced. However, there is no transition period in between where the result is only in the process of coming into existence and the cause is in the process of going out of existence, where the cause and result could interact. Things either exist or they do not. There is no quasi-existence in between where things "sort of" exist.

How can something that is nonexistent become something that is existent?

You can have the idea of the sound of a finger snap before it is produced, but that is just a thought, it is not the sound. Likewise, you can have the idea that the sound went from nonexistence to existence, but that is also just a thought. We won't find anything that corresponds to it. The only thing we can really say is that while the sound appears, it is appearing, and while it is not appearing, it is not. Therefore, the sound is merely an appearance.

To briefly look at the last two cases, it is impossible for results to be *both* existing and not existing, because these two are mutually exclusive, and the same is true when it comes to something being *neither* existing nor not existing. There are no phenomena that are both existing and not existing, and there are also no phenomena that are neither existing nor not existing.

The Analysis of Both Causes and Results

The fourth Middle Way reasoning, the analysis of both causes and results together, looks at causality from yet another angle. This reasoning says that if causes and results really exist, then one of the following must apply:

- One cause produces one result.
- One cause produces many results.
- Many causes produce one result.
- Many causes produce many results.

This reasoning highlights the way concepts impute causes and results to appearances that do not truly exist as unitary things.

Imagine you are driving a car down a busy street in a big city. As you approach an intersection, the traffic light turns red. Since you are a sensible, law-abiding citizen, you stop the car before reaching the intersection. What is the cause-and-effect relationship in this situation? We might think, for example, that one cause—the light turning red—produces one result—stopping the car.

At this point I have to confess that I had a short career during my college years as a rabid behavioral psychologist. During that time, I did a lot of research that involved rats pressing levers for water, and pigeons pecking at illuminated disks for food. The pigeon experiments usually involved changing the color, or some other visual aspect of the disks, to see how the pigeons responded. Thinking about the light-turning-red, driver-braking-car scenario brings that Skinnerian* phase of my life back like heartburn after a rich, spicy meal.

One cause cannot produce one result, as we can easily see when we investigate what happens when the traffic light changes color. When the light turns red, many results occur: your foot moves from the gas peddle to the brake and starts applying pressure, your body presses into the back of the seat, the images of movement around you decelerate, and the car slows to a halt, to name a few.

Can it be that one cause produces many results? This also is not possible, because it is not just the light turning red that causes all these results. Think about all the training you went through to learn that "red means stop and green means go," and all the practice you needed to develop the skills to control a vehicle. These trainings are causes, seeing the intersection and noticing the colors of the light are causes, and so on. Obviously, there are many causes involved, but they do not produce one result, as we have already seen.

Many causes cannot produce many results either, because, as

---

* B. F. (Burrhus Frederic) Skinner was an American psychologist who developed the behaviorist school of experimental psychology, which explains human and animal behavior in terms of histories of reinforcement and punishment.

we have seen, causes can be infinitely subdivided, and results can be infinitely subdivided, so no definite connections can be established between any unitary cause and any unitary result.

The analysis of both causes and results together shows that the appearance of causality is merely imputed: genuine reality is free from these concepts. Therefore, causes and results do not truly exist, and if causes and results do not truly exist, phenomena do not truly exist.

Beyond developing our confidence in the emptiness of phenomena, there is another benefit that comes from contemplating this reasoning: it can help us to understand the workings of karma. Usually, when we think about karma, we imagine that one cause does produce one result. This reasoning shows that karma is more subtle and complex than we imagine. It is only confused conceptuality that divides up the expanse of reality into single causes producing single results.

INTERDEPENDENCE

The first four Middle Way reasonings eliminate the extreme views of existence. However, they do not eliminate the extreme view of nonexistence. The fifth Middle Way reasoning, the analysis of interdependence, eliminates both extreme views—that of existence and that of nonexistence. Because of this, it is known as "the king of reasonings." This reasoning says that if phenomena truly existed, they would have to exist independently, from their own side, but since phenomena are interdependent and not independent, they do not truly exist. Because they are interdependent, they are also not nonexistent: they appear in dependence on their causes and conditions.

Interdependence is a translation of the Sanskrit word *pratitya-samutpada*, which the Tibetans translated as *tendrel*. Other English translations for these terms are "dependent arising," "interdependent origination," "dependently related," and "coincident."

A simple way to understand that phenomena arise dependently is to see that their arising always depends on a perceiver. You can think that there is something that isn't being perceived, but such a thing can never be found. It is only from the perspective of thought that we can have the idea that a tree could fall in a forest with no one to hear it. From the perspective of genuine reality, such a thing can never happen—it is strictly imaginary. From the perspective of genuine reality, trees do not fall in forests, because trees and forests are just conceptual imputations and do not exist from their own side. Since whatever phenomenon we may conceive of is just that—a concept—they simply do not exist independently of our concepts of them.

Furthermore, phenomena are dependent in terms of their origin because they depend on causes and conditions to arise. As we saw in the analysis of causes, nothing arises from truly existent causes, and yet phenomena do appear when appropriate causes and conditions gather. These causes and conditions in turn depend on other causes and conditions. This network of dependence is limitless. Phenomena cannot be traced back to anything independent. Therefore, no truly existent cause for them can be found, and so they do not truly exist.

Nagarjuna also explained how phenomena depend on each other for their existence, and therefore do not truly existent. For example, happiness exists only in dependence upon unhappiness, but unhappiness itself cannot exist without depending on happiness. Thus, happiness and unhappiness are dependently existent, and so not truly existent. As Nagarjuna writes:

> If something exists in dependence upon something
> else,
> But that thing upon which it depends

Must also depend upon it,
Then which one of these exists in dependence upon
   which?[1]

Mipham Gyamtso illustrates this predicament with the image of two rocking boats, tied together on the high seas: since neither of the boats is steady to begin with, neither can be used to steady the other.

Dependent arising is a difficult pill to swallow, because we generally think, "There must be something there or else nothing would ever appear!" At a gut level we are convinced that truly existent substantial results must come from truly existent substantial causes. The analysis of interdependence shows that empty causes produce empty results. Even though all phenomena are empty and lack true existence, they do appear, but the way they appear is like illusions, like dreams, like mirages, like movies. It would be good to contemplate Chandrakirti's verse explaining this:

> Empty things, like reflections and so forth,
> Are known to arise due to the coming together of causes
>   and conditions.
> Just as it is that from a reflection or some other empty
>   phenomenon,
> A consciousness beholding the image of that arises,
> So it is that even though all things are empty,
> From their empty causes and conditions they vividly
>   arise.[2]

Nagarjuna explained that if things were not empty, and they truly existed from their own side, with their own nature, they would be permanent and could never change. Therefore arising would be impossible. One of the most important verses in *The Fundamental Wisdom of the Middle Way* drives this point home:

If emptiness is possible,
Then everything is possible,
But if emptiness is impossible,
Then nothing else is possible either.[3]

Another way to look at the interdependence of phenomena is in terms of their characteristics. For example, it is easy to see that "small" depends on "large." Something is only small if something else is large. A ferryboat is small compared to an aircraft carrier. Compared to a rowboat, the same ferryboat is large. Small cannot exist independently of large. They are imputed in dependence on each other. In other words, characteristics do not exist from the side of the object.

"Other" is dependent on "self." I consider some phenomena to be "me" and some phenomena to be "other." When "you" look at the same phenomena, it is easy to see that these are just dependent imputations: my "me" is your "other."

Nothing exists independently. Nagarjuna wrote:

Whatever is dependently arisen
Is explained to be emptiness.
Its existence is imputed in dependence upon something
    else,
And this is the path of the Middle Way.[4]

On a clear night, with a full moon, standing by a still lake, a person with clear vision might see a water-moon, a mere reflection. A water-moon is an excellent example of dependent arising. There is no moon in the lake and yet its image appears clearly. The self is just like a water-moon. So, too, are all phenomena.

In one of his songs Milarepa sang:

Here on Künsal Rinchen Drak, the precious peak where
    all is clear,
I remember appearances are examples of impermanence.
I see sense pleasures as a mirage, this life like a dream
    and an illusion,
And I cultivate compassion for all who do not know this.
I eat the food of empty space, I meditate without dis-
    traction,
I have different experiences, just about anything can
    happen!
E ma, the phenomena of the three realms of samsara,
While not existing, they appear, how incredibly
    amazing![5]

This is something we need to contemplate again and again.

15

THE ANALYSIS OF THE
AUTOMOBILE

E GOLESSNESS IS REALIZED in stages. There are different ways of explaining this progression, which probably come from emphasizing different methods for making the journey. At least that is my hunch.

According to the more common system, presented by Asanga, first we realize the selflessness, or egolessness, of the individual. This is recognizing that there is no self in the skandhas.* Ego or self is just imputed to exist by thought. This is what shravaka arhats realize.† Egolessness of the individual produces liberation from suffering.

---

* See chapter 5 for an explanation of how this is done.

† There are many ways to classify Buddhist yanas or vehicles. One system presents three vehicles: the shravakayana, or vehicle of hearers; the pratyeka-buddhayana, or vehicle of solitary realizers; and the bodhisattvayana, or vehicle of bodhisattvas. This system describes four types of noble beings who realize the fruitions of these vehicles: shravaka arhats realize the fruition of the shravakayana; pratyekabuddha arhats realize the fruition of the pratyekabuddhayana; bodhisattvas attain the *bhumis*; and *buddhas* complete the paths and levels and attain non-abiding nirvana.

Next we realize the selflessness of phenomena. First, half of the selflessness of phenomena is realized by seeing that perceived objects are empty of any essence. Since it includes all of the egolessness of the individual, and half of the egolessness of dharmas, this stage is sometimes called "one-and-a-half–fold egolessness." This is what pratyekabuddha arhats realize.

Finally, we realize that the perceiving subjects are also emptiness. This is "twofold egolessness," and is what noble bodhisattvas and buddhas realize. Twofold egolessness produces both liberation and omniscience.

Chandrakirti, interpreting Nagarjuna, presents twofold egolessness in a different way, emphasizing first the selflessness of phenomena. He says that selflessness of the individual can't be realized without recognizing the selflessness of phenomena, and once phenomenal selflessness has been understood, it is easy to teach the selflessness of the individual. In this presentation, the level of realization of the different noble beings depends on the extent of their realization of the selflessness of phenomena. In *Entering the Middle Way*, Chandrakirti uses an elegant seven-point analysis to point out individual selflessness. Since we have contemplated the five great reasonings of the Middle Way that refute the self of phenomena, it would now be good to examine Chandrakirti's analysis of the selflessness of the individual.

The section of *Entering the Middle Way* on the selflessness of the individual begins with a verse that explains why we need to refute the self:

> Seeing that all faults and afflictions without exception
> Arise from the view of the transitory collection,
> And understanding that the object of that view is the
>   "self,"
> Yogis refute the self.[1]

What are the "faults and afflictions"? The faults are birth, old age, sickness, death, and misery. The afflictions are attachment, anger, stupidity, and so on. All of these faults and afflictions arise from "the view of the transitory collection." What is this view? It is various ways the transitory collection, or skandhas, or aggregates, are taken to be a self. Since this grasping at the transitory collection causes such afflictions and misery, it makes sense to refute the self that is the basis for this view.

Parts of the following investigation will seem familiar from earlier chapters, but this time we will proceed along a slightly different path. In any event, individual egolessness is something we need to contemplate again and again, so repeating this is definitely worthwhile.

To begin with, simply contemplate how you experience ego:

See if you can find anything, anywhere, that corresponds with the following: a personality, a perceiver, an experiencer, a soul, a doer, an ego. Look inside and look outside. What is the self like? Is the self something altogether inexpressible?

If you can't find anything at all, that's fine: that is egolessness of the individual. If you do find something that seems to be an ego, that's also fine. You have something to work with, and this book won't be a complete waste of time and money!

Now contemplate whether the self is the same as the skandhas or different from the skandhas. You might need to refresh your understanding of the skandhas by looking back at chapter 5. Briefly, the five skandhas are as follows: forms, feelings, discriminations, formations, and consciousnesses. See if the self is something different from these skandhas:

If the self is different from the skandhas, it is not form, it is not feelings, it is not discriminations, it is not formations, and it is not consciousness. All of these are experienced, but can you find something else? Is there anything other than the experiences themselves? What would a self be like that is not made up of the skandhas?

If we were able to apprehend the self and the skandhas distinctly, we could say that there is a self that is different from the skandhas. But the truth is we don't observe anything other than the skandhas. Everything we experience falls into these five "heaps." For example, you never actually see one thing that is a self possessing another thing that is the body. Chandrakirti concludes:

> Therefore, there is no self different from the aggregates,
> Because apart from the aggregates, nothing is perceived
>   to be a self.[2]

Next, since the self is not different from the skandhas, see if the self is the same as the skandhas.

Is the self made of form, feelings, discriminations, formations, consciousnesses? Is it a combination of these, or is it only one of them by itself?

Some people believe that all five skandhas are the self. Others believe that only mind is the self. But since there are many skandhas, and each skandha is a heap of endlessly changing phenomena, if the self were the skandhas, there would be many selves. If, on the other hand, the self is only the mind, since mind is also many—for example, eye consciousnesses, ear consciousnesses, nose consciousnesses, tongue consciousnesses, body consciousnesses, mental consciousnesses—there would still be many selves. This contradicts our experience that the self is one thing. Therefore, Chandrakirti concludes:

> If the aggregates were the self,
> Since there are many aggregates, there would be that
>   many selves.[3]

You might think that it is not the actual skandhas, but the continuum of the skandhas, or perhaps the collection of the skandhas, that is the basis for the self. But we have already discussed continua and collections at length, and we know they are just imputations. As Chandrakirti remarks:

> Should you say, "In reality there is a continuum, so there
>   is no fault,"
> Earlier analysis has shown the faults of positing that a
>   continuum exists.
> Therefore, it would be illogical for the self to be either
>   the five aggregates or mind alone.[4]

Finally, you might conclude that even though the self is not the same as the skandhas, and it is not different from the skandhas, that doesn't mean it does not exist: the self could be inexpressible. It could exist in a way that can't be described as either the same as the skandhas or different from them. The self could be ineffable. However, there is no such thing as something that is neither the same as nor different from something else. If the self truly exists, it would have to be one or the other. As Chandrakirti writes:

Just as mind is not understood to be inexpressible in
    relation to body,
Things which exist are not inexpressible.
Therefore, if the self existed as a thing,
It, like mind, would not be inexpressible.[5]

This investigation shows that however we conceive of it, the
self does not truly exist. Rather, the self is merely imputed—
sometimes on the basis of the elements, sometimes on the basis
of the sense organs, sometimes on the basis of mind and mental
events, and sometimes on the basis of the skandhas. Chandrakirti
sums this up in two verses:

The Mighty One taught that the self is imputed to exist
    in dependence upon
The six elements: earth, water, fire, air, consciousness,
    and space,
And the six supports for contact:
The eye, ear, nose, and so forth.

At other times, we impute the self's existence in depend-
    ence upon mind and mental events, the Buddha
    definitively taught.
Therefore, the self is not different from the aggregates,
    nor is it the aggregates themselves, nor is it the collec-
    tion of them,
And therefore, no matter what its base of reference,
The mind thinking "self" is illogical.[6]

The View of the Transitory Collection

By repeatedly contemplating in this way, you will be able to gain
confidence that thinking "I" and "mine" is illogical. To go fur-

ther with this investigation of selflessness, we will explore the view of the transitory collection.

The view of the transitory collection describes various ways the skandhas are taken to be a self. There are four main ways this is done:

- The first is that *we are the phenomena*, thinking, "This ___ is me."
- The second is that *we possess the phenomena*, thinking, "This is my ___."
- The third is that *we are supported by the phenomena*, thinking, "I exist based on ___."
- The fourth is that *the phenomena are supported by us*, thinking, "___ exists based on me."

The first one is thinking that the self is the same thing as the phenomena. The other three imagine that the self and phenomena are different entities. We could contemplate examples of these four to feel the differences in the relationships:

Examples of the first: "I am this body and mind"; "I am sick"; "I am these five skandhas."

Examples of the second: "This is my anger"; "I have a cold"; "I have five skandhas."

Examples of the third: "I am in this body"; "I am based on my brain"; "The five skandhas support my existence."

Examples of the fourth: "Thoughts arise from me"; "This body is part of me"; "The five skandhas are based on me."

It is important to note that these are not just linguistic differences. They are different ways of imputing or conceiving of the self. We do this constantly. Since there are five skandhas, and each of the four relationships can apply to each skandha, collectively these twenty views are known as "the lofty peaks of the mountainous view of the transitory collection."

The image of a mountain with twenty peaks works well. Ego is not lots of individual things, like many different mountains, nor is it a monolith, like one great big peak. If ego were many different things, it would have no continuity; and if it were a monolith, it would be easy to refute. Because it is imputed in very flexible ways, ego is very durable. It is constantly recasting itself, and yet it covers all the gaps. It is like a guerilla army that pops up all over the place and can't be pinned down. One moment "I" is the thinker; the next moment "I" has a headache; the next moment "I" is an ear consciousness; and next, "my" confusion overwhelms me. It is a very flexible system of constantly changing views with a continuous underlying feeling of its own existence.

To fully overcome all faults and afflictions, we need to develop the prajna that realizes selflessness. This cuts through the view of self and the twenty lofty peaks at the same time. Chandrakirti writes:

> The vajra-like realization of selflessness
> Destroys the apprehension of "self," and at the same
>   time,
> The twenty lofty peaks of the mountainous view of the
>   transitory collection
> Are completely destroyed as well.[7]

Cars and Carts

Because ego is so deeply rooted and covers such a diverse range of phenomena, it is extremely difficult to see how we impute the self onto the skandhas. To vividly demonstrate this process,

Chandrakirti gives a practical external example of imputation using a seven-point analysis. He uses a cart or chariot for this demonstration, but we can use an automobile.

There are seven points in Chandrakirti's analysis because, to cover all the bases, he adds three more relationships to the four we just discussed. These three are:

- The self, or the automobile, is something different from its parts.
- The self, or the automobile, is the mere collection of its parts.
- The self, or the automobile, is the shape of its parts.

These fifteen verses make such an excellent contemplation that I include them without further commentary. If you wrestle with them for a while, you should be able to see how mind projects the existence of things onto mere appearances, and understand that the self is just a projection.

The automobile is not something different than
    its parts,
It is not the same as its parts, it does not possess its
    parts,
It does not depend on its parts, the parts do not
    depend on it,
It is not the mere collection of its parts, nor is it
    the parts' shape.

If the mere collection of the parts were the
    automobile,
A heap of disassembled parts would still be an
    automobile.
And since there is no possessor of the parts, there
    can be no parts,

So the mere shape of the parts cannot be the automobile, either!

If you say the parts each have the same shape they
    had when they were separate,
Meaning that when they are thought to be an
    automobile, their shapes have not undergone
    any change,
Then just as there was no automobile when they
    were disassembled,
So when assembled there is no automobile, either.

If at the time there is an automobile
The wheels and so forth had different shapes than
    before they were assembled,
That difference would be perceivable.
Since it is not, the mere shape is not the automobile.

Even in your tradition, the "collection" does not
    exist substantially at all,
And therefore, the shape of the parts is not the
    shape of the parts' collection.
How could something like shape, suitable to be
    seen,
Exist in dependence upon something that does
    not exist at all?

Just as you assert the "collection" to be unreal, a
    mere imputation,
So it is that in dependence upon unreal causes
Appear the images of results that are unreal by
    nature.
Know the arising of everything to be just like this.

Thus it is illogical for the mind to superimpose the
  existence of an automobile*
Onto the form abiding in that way.
Since the form is unarisen, it does not exist.
Therefore, the automobile cannot be the form's
  shape.

Although it is true that both in terms of suchness
  and conventional reality,
When analyzed, automobiles and so forth cannot
  be found to exist in any of the seven ways,
In the world itself where there is no analysis,
Things are imputed to exist in dependence upon
  their parts.

Beings say, "That automobile has parts, it has
  sections,
That automobile can do things."
Individuals, moreover, are known to be
  "appropriators."
Therefore, do not destroy the relative appearances
  commonly known in the world.

How could that which does not exist in any of the
  seven ways be said to exist?
The yogis find no such existence.
Through this realization, they easily engage in
  suchness,

---

* Chandrakirti switched from cart to vase in the original verse because he
was giving an illogical consequence of an opponent's reasoning using a
vase as the example. Vases and pillars were used quite frequently as examples in Buddhist logical debates. For our contemplation, an automobile
works better.

And therefore, we must assert that the existence
of things is only from the perspective of no
analysis.

If the automobile itself does not exist,
Then since there is no possessor of the parts, the
parts do not exist, either!
Just as if fire burned the automobile, its parts
would also cease to exist,
So when the fire of knowledge burns the parts-
possessor, it burns the parts as well.

Similarly, the five aggregates, the six elements and
the six sources of consciousnesses are renowned
in the world,
And in dependence upon them, the self is asserted
to be their appropriator.
What are appropriated are the aggregates and so
forth,
And the self is also asserted to be an agent of
action.

Since the self is not a thing, it is neither changing
nor unchanging,
It is not born and it does not die,
It is neither permanent, impermanent, both, nor
neither,
And it is neither the same nor different from the
aggregates.

Wandering beings constantly cling to some basis as
being "me,"
And then conceive of other things as being "mine."

The self that they have imagined and that is
    renowned in the world
Exists only when there is no analysis; the thought
    of it arises from bewilderment.

If there is no actor, there is no object of action.
Therefore, if there is no self, there is nothing that
    could be said to belong to the self.
Seeing the emptiness of "me" and "mine"
The yogis are completely liberated.[8]

16

SHENTONG MADHYAMAKA

A T THE END OF THE 1970s, a young Kagyu lineage holder was preparing for his first teaching tour of North America. Nervous about how to present the dharma in such a different world, he went to his guru, the sixteenth Gyalwang Karmapa, to ask how he should approach these Westerners. The Karmapa laughed and said, "Tell them they are basically good!" After a short pause he added, "If they want to know more—tell them they are buddhas!"

The Karmapa's message was that the final fruit of the path is the wisdom that has always been with us. It is not nothingness. After the Buddha taught the essencelessness of all phenomena in the second turning of the wheel of dharma, he taught the *tathagata-garbha*, or buddha nature, in the third turning. Tathagata-garbha means that all sentient beings, from the smallest insect to the most realized human, have this wisdom nature, and have had this nature from beginningless time. Therefore, the purpose of the path is to reveal buddhahood, not to create it. From this perspective, it does not make sense to say that buddhahood is produced by journeying along the path. If buddhahood was a product, it would be something compounded and subject to decay.

It is hard to reconcile buddha nature, or original wisdom,

with our current samsaric experience. To help us understand this idea, the tathagata-garbha teachings use images or analogies to describe what this is like. One is that buddha nature is like the sun when it is behind a thick bank of clouds. It might not look like the sun is shining, but whether there are clouds in the sky or not, the sun is always there. In the same way, whether there is confusion in our minds or not, the sun of wisdom is always shining. Clouds are temporary, or incidental, coverings. The sun is permanent. Confusion is temporary, or incidental; it is not part of our basic being. Wisdom *is* our basic being. It is unstained by temporary faults, just as the sun is unstained by passing clouds.

Another analogy for buddha nature is the way butter is contained within milk. Until the cream is skimmed and churned, the butter is hidden. In the same way, wisdom is concealed within our minds by cognitive and *klesha* obscurations. When these temporary stains are removed, the wisdom manifests. A third analogy is the gold that exists within gold ore but is obscured by dross. When the ore is refined, the impurities are removed and the pure gold manifests. In the same way, when the minds of beings are refined by the path, buddha nature manifests. It would be good to contemplate these three analogies.

You might wonder why the third-turning teachings are necessary, since the second-turning teachings are perfectly capable of opening the door to genuine reality. Complete freedom from conceptual contrivance, which is the ultimate view of the second turning, should allow the clear-light nature of mind to shine like the sun emerging from behind clouds. However, the wisdom mind is difficult to recognize because it is extremely subtle. Since training in the second-turning teachings involves much analysis and strong tendencies for negating whatever arises, it can be difficult to completely let go and rest the mind in its own nature. The subtle movement of the analyzing mind itself obscures the clear-light nature. Developing confidence in buddha nature is the antidote for such activity. As Khenpo Tsültrim Gyamtso explains in *Progressive Stages of Meditation on Emptiness*:

> The purpose of teaching the Tathagata-garbha is to give the meditator confidence that he already has Buddha Nature. Without such confidence it is very difficult to fully rest the mind free from all conceptual contrivance, because there is always a subtle tendency to try to remove or achieve something.[1]

To sum this section up, a famous line from the *Hevajra Tantra* says:

> All sentient beings are buddhas with stains.

THE UTTARATANTRA-SHASTRA

The protector Maitreya taught buddha nature extensively in the *Uttaratantra-shastra*,* which was recorded by the noble bodhisattva Asanga. In it, buddha nature is compared to a great hidden treasure that can overcome all impoverishment:

> If an inexhaustible treasure were buried
> in the ground beneath a poor man's house,
> the man would not know of it, and the treasure
> would not speak and tell him "I am here!"
>
> Likewise a precious treasure is contained in each being's
>   mind. This is its true state,

---

* The title of the *Mahayana Uttaratantra Shastra* has been translated into English as *The Highest Continuum*, *The Changeless Nature*, and *The Treatise on Buddha Nature*.

Which is free from defilement. Nothing is to be added
and nothing to be removed.
Nevertheless, since they do not realize this, sentient
beings
continuously undergo the manifold sufferings of
deprivation.[2]

The purpose of the path is to reveal this treasure to us. The *Uttaratantra* gives three reasons why all sentient beings have buddha nature, ten points that explain its qualities, and nine metaphors for the way sentient beings' minds are, by nature, wisdom, while temporarily being obscured by defilements.

The three reasons given to explain that all sentient beings have buddha nature are: First, since the expanse of reality is completely pervaded by buddha wisdom, there can be no other basis for sentient beings. Second, since this wisdom is primordially free from duality, nothing is outside of it. Third, since all beings wish to escape suffering and attain peace, all have the seed or disposition toward buddhahood. The *Uttaratantra* gives these reasons in two verses:

The perfect buddhakaya is all-embracing,
suchness cannot be differentiated,
and all beings have the disposition.
Thus they always have buddha nature.

The Buddha has said that all beings have buddha
nature
"since buddha wisdom is always present within the
assembly of beings,
since this undefiled nature is free from duality,
and since the disposition to buddhahood has been named
after its fruit."[3]

The last point is elaborated upon in a third verse a little farther on in the text:

If the buddha element were not present,
there would be no remorse over suffering.
There would be no longing for nirvana,
nor striving and devotion towards this aim.[4]

The ten-point presentation of the qualities of buddha nature is extensive. We will look at some of the key verses (which make good contemplations). The first one presents the expansiveness of buddha wisdom. This is important because we usually conceive of ego as bound by location and time. In fact, the wisdom mind is completely without limit. When we are released from the temporary defilements of concepts and kleshas, we discover the undefiled expanse:

Just as space, which is by nature free from thought,
pervades everything,
the undefiled expanse, which is the nature of mind,
is all-pervading.[5]

The next verse describes the way stains are adventitious (incidental, not inherent), whereas buddha nature is permanent and unchanging. This counteracts our usual understanding that we are made up of stains, that they are basic to our makeup. Instead, what *is* basic is wisdom, which needs no transformation. It merely needs to be released from temporary obscurations:

Having faults that are adventitious
and qualities that are its nature,
it is afterwards the same as before.
This is dharmata ever unchanging.[6]

The next verse explains that the source of all the obscurations is incorrect or mistaken thought. The way the obscurations are removed is by transforming our thinking. This allows the clear and luminous nature of mind to shine forth:

This clear and luminous nature of mind
is as changeless as space. It is not afflicted
by desire and so on, the adventitious stains,
which are sprung from incorrect thoughts.[7]

To show how profound buddha nature is, the *Uttaratantra* explains that it cannot be experienced through study, it cannot be experienced through contemplation, and it cannot be experienced through conventional meditation, since all of these involve conceptuality. The only way to experience the wisdom mind is to let mind rest in its own nature:

Being subtle it is not an object for study.
Being absolute it cannot be reflected upon.
Dharmata is deep. Hence it is not an object
for any worldly meditation and so on.[8]

EMPTY-OF-SELF OR EMPTY-OF-OTHER

That the nature of mind is not mere emptiness, but luminosity and emptiness inseparable, is the distinguishing feature of this final Middle Way school, the Shentong Madhyamaka, or empty-of-other Middle Way. Luminosity-emptiness is sometimes referred to as "emptiness endowed with the supreme of all characteristics." It is emptiness endowed with the wisdoms and buddha qualities. Jamgön Kongtrul was an articulate proponent of Shentong Madhyamaka, and this section is based on his presentation in *The Treasury of Knowledge*.

In previous chapters, we investigated the Middle Way reasonings that refute the true existence of all outer and inner phenomena. These reasonings definitely demonstrate that all phenomena are empty, have no nature, and have no essence. All phenomena are empty of whatever we conceive them to be. All are free from conceptual fabrications. All are Rangtong—empty-of-self. Nevertheless, from the Shentong point of view, this cannot be the final word on genuine reality. As Jamgön Kongtrul writes:

> This system states, "It is explained clearly that sutras teaching that all phenomena have no inherent nature (nihsvabhava, ngo bo nyid med pa) are not to be taken literally. Anyone who accepts such statements as literal is a propounder of nihilism."[9]

The Shentong explanation of emptiness avoids this dead end. Shentongpas, like all Madhyamikas, agree that genuine reality is empty of conceptual fabrications, but they go on to assert that genuine reality is not empty of non-dual wisdom. This is what the term *Shentong*, or empty-of-other, actually means. Genuine reality is empty of conceptual fabrications, which are incidental or *other*, but it is not empty of the wisdom that is its nature.

In his commentary on Maitreya's *Ornament of the Mahayana Sutras*, Mipham Gyamtso points out that it is necessary to assert self-aware wisdom, otherwise it is impossible to explain the basis for realization, the buddha kayas, wisdoms, and buddha activity:

> If there were no intuitive, reflexively aware wisdom, also referred to as the luminous mind, it would not be possible for there to be a mind that realizes the truth of dharmata on the path of learning. This would also mean that buddhas would have no omniscient wisdom when they have

attained nirvana without remainder, which is the path of
no more learning; in which case, buddhahood would not
differ from the Hinayana nirvana, which is like the extin-
guishing of a candle flame. If that were the case, how
could anything be said about the kayas, wisdoms, and inex-
haustible activity of a buddha?

Consequently, although the founders of the great systems of Chittamatra and Madhyamaka present the paths of
the profound and vast dharma in ways that seem to differ,
their final thought arrives at the same point in the expanse
of wisdom. If we understand this crucial point, we will see
the excellence of both these systems.[10]

THE THREE NATURES IN SHENTONG

The three natures are the dependent nature, the imaginary
nature, and the perfectly existent nature. We discussed the Chittamatra presentation of the three natures in chapter 9. Shentongpas also use the three natures to distinguish between apparent
reality and genuine reality. Their presentation is similar to that
found in the Chittamatra, but with an important difference. Both
say that genuine reality is the perfectly existent nature. Chittamatrins say that the perfectly existent nature is the dependent nature
free from the imaginary nature. They say this pure dependent
nature is consciousness. Shentongpas say that the perfectly existent nature is not consciousness but wisdom, and that it is free
from *both* the dependent nature and the imaginary nature.
Jamgön Kongtrul summarizes the Shentong view this way:

> The imaginary and dependent aspects are apparent
>   reality,
> The perfectly existent nature, self-aware, original wisdom
>   is genuine.
> This is the Empty-of-Other presentation.[11]

What is imagined and what depends on causes and conditions only appear to exist. What is genuine is self-aware wisdom, buddha nature. This wisdom does not arise or cease, but exists continually. It is not possible to experience this wisdom conventionally, because it is beyond the reach of fabrications. That buddha nature is utterly beyond the conceptual mind is a key point.

Conventionally, on the level of apparent reality, the imaginary nature does not exist—it is just imaginary. Conventionally, the dependent nature does exist—it appears. Conventionally, the perfectly existent nature does not exist—it cannot be experienced by any conventional mind.

Ultimately, on the level of genuine reality, the imaginary nature and the dependent nature do not exist—they are not found at all. Ultimately, the perfectly existent nature does exist—it knows itself, by itself. Another verse from *The Treasury of Knowledge* says:

> The imagined nature is nonexistent; the dependent exists
> conventionally.
> The consummate does not exist conventionally but does
> exist ultimately.[12]

THREE EXISTENCES, THREE EMPTINESSES, AND THREE INHERENT ABSENCES

To take this further, the Shentong explanation of the three natures very precisely distinguishes how each nature exists, how each nature is empty, and how each nature lacks an inherent essence. This is an important and subtle presentation that is worth contemplating.

Each of the natures exists in the following way: The imaginary nature exists nominally as a name or a sign—for example, in a dream of Dorothy and the Tin Woodsman from *The Wizard of*

Oz, the imaginary nature exists merely as these two names. The dependent nature exists substantially as mere appearance—in the dream, images that are the basis of imputing the names Dorothy and the Tin Woodsman do appear. The perfectly existent nature does not exist in either of these ways, but does exist in a way that is beyond both existence and nonexistence—it is the basic ground from which the dream arises.

Each of the natures is empty in the following way: The imaginary nature is empty as a nonexistent—you don't find the real Dorothy and the real Tin Woodsman anywhere. The dependent nature is empty as an existent—the dream of Dorothy and the Tin Woodsman appears, while being empty of self-nature. The perfectly existent nature is ultimate emptiness, which is the inseparability of luminosity and emptiness—it can never be established as anything.

Finally, each of the natures lacks an inherent essence in the following way: The imaginary nature lacks any inherent characteristics—the real Dorothy and the real Tin Woodsman are not tall or short, happy or sad, beautiful or ugly, because they do not exist. The dependent nature is the inherent absence of arising—the dream Dorothy and the dream Tin Woodsman don't come from anywhere and don't go anywhere. The perfectly existent nature is the ultimate absence of essence—it cannot be grasped by any concept.

If you understand existence, nonexistence, and inherent absence in these ways, you will understand the basis for confusion in samsara, and liberation in nirvana. Jamgön Kongtrul gives a verse for these that is easy to contemplate:

These three characteristics are imputedly existent, substantially existent, and existent without conceptual elaborations.
They are the emptiness of the nonexistent, the

emptiness of the existent, and the ultimate
emptiness.

They are the inherent absence of characteristics, the
inherent absence of arising, and the ultimate
inherent absence.[13]

THE FINAL INTENTION OF THE MAHAYANA

As you can see from this discussion of buddha nature, we have
arrived at the outer limit of what can be contemplated: it's all
meditation from here. The tathagata-garbha teachings form a
bridge between the sutras and the tantras. Tantra, or vajrayana, is
known as "the fruitional vehicle" because it takes the fruition—
buddha nature, or the true nature of mind—as the path.

Having climbed the last great peak of sutrayana views, this is a
good vantage point from which to look back at the ground we
have covered. From here we can clearly see the two main mahayana traditions. The tradition of Maitreya and Asanga includes
the branches known as Chittamatra, Yogachara, and Shentong,
and emphasizes the nondual nature of self-aware wisdom.

The tradition of Nagarjuna and Chandrakirti includes the
branches known as Svatantrika and Prasangika, and emphasizes
the emptiness and original purity of all phenomena. Both traditions teach the selflessness of persons.

It is often said that the Middle Way teachings of Nagarjuna's
tradition are most important at the time of training in the view,
because they provide extensive methods for analyzing and investigating. The teachings of Maitreya's tradition are most important
at the time of meditating on the nature of mind, because they
point out the fruition. Both are necessary.

You should definitely understand that the final views of these two traditions do not differ. It is wonderful to be passionate about different aspects of the teachings. My enthusiasm certainly bounced around as I worked on various sections of this book. However, passion and enthusiasm can slide into bias and sectarianism. These only serve to reinforce ego and cut us off from the sources of realization. Seeing how these traditions complement each other is a great remedy for bias.

In *The Ocean of Texts of Reasoning*, the seventh Karmapa, Chödrak Gyamtso, showed how to harmonize the final views of these traditions:

> The great Yogachara Centrists* who follow noble As-anga and his brother† mainly teach the wisdom that real-izes self-aware, self-luminous mind by ascertaining that the dualistic appearances of apprehender and apprehended that obscure true reality are not established in the way they appear.
>
> Noble Nagarjuna and his spiritual heirs mainly teach that the nature of luminous mind abides as emptiness by thoroughly analyzing the clinging to real existence and its objects that obscure true reality through the great Centrist arguments. In this way, they ascertain that this clinging and its objects are without nature.
>
> Both systems do not differ in teaching the final true reality, since this very nature of luminous mind primor-dially is emptiness, and this emptiness primordially abides as the essential character of luminosity.[14]

Jamgön Kongtrul describes the benefits of unbiasedness in the following quotation from *The Treasury of Knowledge*:

---

* This is another name for Shentong Madhyamikas.
† Vasubandhu.

The Instruction which Profoundly Comprehends
as One the Thought of the Two Chariots

> Having understood the system of each of the founders,
>   the Two Chariots,
> If you profoundly comprehend their thought as the
>   same, you will be liberated from the faults of
>   superimposition and denial
> And obtain flawless vision of the ultimate view of the
>   sutras and tantras.

Both Nagarjuna and Asanga, the Two Great Chari-oteers, who beautifully adorn this world, were undeniably predicted by the Victorious One and indisputably abide on the noble levels. There is absolutely no difference of superiority and inferiority between their thought. . . . If you profoundly comprehend that their ultimate intention is identical, then you will be liberated from the myriad faults of superimposition and denial and attain flawless vision of the ultimate view of the sutras and the tantras. Through meditation, reflection on the meaning and so forth, you realize in relation to the texts of Nagarjuna and Asanga, the cutting through of mental elaborations such as one of the traditions being provisional and the other ultimate. Untouched by the faults of seeing contradictions in relation to the views of the sutra and vajrayana, you will realize unmistakably the mind of the Buddha which is liberated from the imputations created by the minds of ordinary individuals.[15]

LAST INTERLUDE

Looking Nakedly, Resting Still
*A song of realization sung by Milarepa
to his student, Megom Repa* *

I the yogi, Milarepa, look nakedly and see the essence
What I see is beyond concept, what I see resembles
    space
Free from motion, resting still—I realize the true nature
All the things there are are empty—their empty essence is
    what I realize
Relaxing loosely, letting go—original wisdom holds its
    ground
In the river of awareness the mud settles down and the
    brightness shines
I take my concepts and throw them away—recollection
    and thoughts are cut
The deep abyss of the six realms has been sealed
    completely—that's over for me now
I know for sure my mind is Buddha, so there's nothing I
    need to gain or achieve

---

* Translated by Ari Goldfield, under the guidance of Khenpo Tsültrim
Gyamtso Rinpoche, from the Tibetan text.

When realization shines from inside, it's like when the
sun's light shines on the night
All my thoughts, the whole collection, and disturbing
states of mind
Without effort, in their own place, disappearing and now
gone.[1]

17

MEDITATION

THERE IS A THREAD that runs through the views we have been contemplating: genuine reality is beyond conception. Since contemplation and investigation involve lots of concepts, they can bring us to understand the genuine, but understanding is not the same as direct experience. To make the crossing, we need to take a leap. This is meditation's role.

All Buddhist schools agree that meditation on genuine reality is free from fabrications, but each school has a different way of describing what that is. Vaibhashikas and Sautrantikas call it the selflessness of persons. Chittamatrins say it is consciousness, free from the duality of perceiver and perceived. Svatantrikas call it the total negation of everything, which is like space. Prasangikas say it is dharmadhatu, free from complexity. Shentongpas describe it as inseparable clarity-emptiness, free from complexity. However it is described, this is what we have to leap into.

Since there are many meditation techniques that serve similar functions, I don't think it is necessary to go into technique here. You probably know how to meditate already, but if not, you can learn about it in other places, preferably from an experienced meditation instructor. Instead, I will present some general points on joining contemplation with meditation.

To begin with, if you don't have a regular, stable practice, you have no base from which to leap. Perhaps the most difficult part of meditation is getting oneself onto the cushion (or wherever you sit). For those of us trying to practice while working in the world, establishing a regular practice is challenging.

After I had been practicing for about fifteen years, I woke up one morning and realized that I didn't have a daily practice. I would do retreats and practice at home, but then wouldn't get around to meditating for days at a time, even though the Buddhist path was the most important thing in my life. Seeing this contradiction caused a wave of embarrassment to crash over me. As I lay in bed feeling shitty, I remembered hearing a friend say that Trungpa Rinpoche had told him to sit for at least ten minutes a day. When he mentioned that, it sounded pretty wimpy, but reflecting back, I realized that no matter how busy I was, there would never be a day where I could honestly say that I couldn't find ten minutes to sit. Before getting out of bed that morning I committed to not let another day go by without practicing for at least ten minutes.

That commitment was surprisingly effective. Sometimes I would come home, tired from work, and force myself to sit for a few minutes. Sometimes, on a business trip, my head would be about to hit the pillow and I would remember I hadn't practiced that day. It might be one o'clock in the morning, but I would spring up in bed and sit there like an idiot. It would be an exaggeration to say that I actually meditated at those times, but I certainly made an effort.

I went ten or fifteen years without missing a day, just because the commitment was so clear-cut. Eventually, I found that practicing had become a habit. Now, not practicing feels as unreasonable as missing morning coffee. While this is hardly in the same league as the life stories of Milarepa, for me it was an important stepping-stone. The point is, you don't need to depend on inspiration to meditate. Inspiration comes and goes. You don't have to be inspired to brush your teeth. You just need to know why it is a good idea and then get into the habit.

After getting onto the cushion, the next hardest thing about developing a regular meditation practice is learning to stay there. Most of us start practicing with enthusiasm and a certain amount of naive optimism. This wears out fairly quickly when we discover the boredom, agitation, emotionality, drowsiness, aches, pains, and general cluelessness that we experience when we begin to sit with ourselves for any length of time. Unfortunately, there is really no way around this. You just have to sit through it.

There are three things that will help you. The first is a certain amount of faith in the dharma, which comes from understanding that this is a reliable path that is worth pursuing. The second is the aspiration to become a good practitioner, which comes from understanding the benefits of meditation. The third is good old-fashioned exertion.

If you keep practicing with your difficulties, eventually things will shift. The things that caused so much discomfort before will begin to recede, and you will have subtle experiences of physical and mental well-being. There is a good Tibetan word for this stage: *shinjang*, which means "suppleness," "pliancy," or "thoroughly trained." This is what we experience when we get over the hump. It is not a great revelation, just a feeling of wholesomeness when we practice.

SHAMATHA

As we discussed in chapter 1, there are two aspects to meditation: resting and looking. The Sanskrit term for the resting aspect is *shamatha*, which means "calm-abiding." The Sanskrit term for the looking aspect is *vipashyana*, which means "superior seeing" or "superior insight." Because you need to pacify the mind before you are able to see anything, the resting aspect is emphasized first.

Most of us find the idea of calm-abiding quite appealing, since on a subtle level, agitation, discursiveness, and distraction are our constant companions. They are such a normal part or our inner environment that most of the time we aren't even aware of them, yet we do often have the feeling that something is wrong. In fact, this is the very nature of samsara: to be driven around and around by the momentum of thoughts and emotions. Shamatha practice is a way to reduce this momentum.

In the beginning, shamatha involves trying to stay with an object of meditation and learning to come back when you stray. This is much more difficult than it seems, and people often feel that meditation is making their minds wilder rather than more calm. The traditional images for the development of shamatha describe this first stage as being like a waterfall, since you are becoming aware of all the cascading thoughts and emotions, which you were previously unaware of. It may not feel like it, but this is a positive sign. It means that you are able to meditate and that your mindfulness is increasing.

Gradually, as you practice more, you start to rest with the object of meditation rather than cling to it. When you do get lost in thought, you learn how to come back to the technique naturally, without struggling. Your mental activity slows down a little. The image for this stage is a river flowing through a gorge. As you become still more familiar with the practice, mental activity slows down further, and your mind feels like a large leisurely flowing river.

Eventually you start to see there are different ways of slowing down. If you are driving too fast in your car, you can hit the brakes or you can simply lift your foot from the gas. When we start to meditate, there is a natural tendency to try to find the brakes, but in the long run we learn that there are no brakes nor anyone to put their foot down. We might succeed at suppressing thoughts and emotions for a while, but at the price of binding the mind further. We start to see that the best way of practicing shamatha is to take your foot off the gas while staying mindful. You learn to rest right within the very things that disturb you. You start to work with the energy of mind rather than struggling against it. This brings stability to your practice. From time to time, your experience of resting is like that of an ocean, which is basically calm despite whatever waves there may be at the surface.

This is the general progression of shamatha. You could continue to practice shamatha until you reach the final stage, which is compared to a candle flame unmoved by wind, but this is neither necessary nor desirable. As mind becomes workable, it is more important to shift your emphasis to the looking aspect, because shamatha alone does not lead to liberation. Vipashyana is where contemplation and meditation intersect.

VIPASHYANA

There are two phases to vipashyana practice. The preparatory phase is the phase of analysis, involving concepts. This is nothing other than what we have been calling contemplation when it is done within the framework of formal meditation practice. The second phase is the actual practice of vipashyana, which is non-conceptual.

The practice is called "superior seeing" because it enables you to see what you have not seen before: the two types of selflessness. You do this by taking the view, which has arisen from listening and contemplating, and applying it to the objects of your meditation. This removes misconceptions about the nature of these phenomena. The view of selflessness is the cause for realizing vipashyana.

You begin the practice by focusing on a meditation object, for example, what you take to be "me." Let us say you are starting with the misconception that your mind is "me." To begin your analysis, you need to clearly bring to mind the object you are examining, which is the *present* mind—not the mind of the past, which is already gone, or the mind of the future, which has not yet arisen. You investigate this present mind using one of the reasonings we have been working with, or by simply asking whether this present mind could possibly be the self. When you come to a clear understanding that there is no self in this mind, you drop all analysis and simply look directly at the present mind. You do not continue to think about it in any way, but rather just look. Looking in this way, you see that this present mind is mere empty appearance, and rest right within this freedom from fabrications. At this point meditation and understanding are unified.

You use the same approach to recognize the emptiness of outer objects. For example, you can start with the misconception that the room you are sitting in truly exists. In order to see that the room's nature is actually emptiness, you take the room as the meditation object and begin by analyzing, perhaps investigating whether the room is one thing or many things. When you come to understand that the room is neither one nor many, and does not truly exist, you drop all analysis and look directly at your present experience of the room. You realize that it is form and emptiness inseparable and rest right within this freedom from fabrications.

Practicing vipashyana when you are angry is especially revealing. Anger is based on the misconception that the object of your anger truly exists. To correct this misconception, you take the object of your anger as the object of meditation and analyze it. When you come to a clear understanding that the object of your anger is just a projection, you look right at that projecting mind and realize that its nature is emptiness and rest right within this freedom from fabrications.

These are ways of recognizing the emptiness of perceived objects. You use the same methods to see the emptiness of the perceiving mind. For example, you have the misconception that the thinker exists. To remove this misconception, you might begin by analyzing the relationship between thoughts and the thinker. When you come to a clear understanding that thoughts are just imputed in dependence on a thinker and the thinker is just imputed in dependence on thoughts, and therefore neither thought nor thinker truly exist, you drop all analysis and look directly at the thinking mind. You realize that the thinking mind is empty and rest right within this freedom from fabrications.

At first, your experience of nonconceptual vipashyana will probably be very brief. The excitement of seeing anything often covers over the insight, and thick habitual patterns of self-clinging quickly kick in to distract you. Gradually, however, through practicing in this way, confidence in selflessness and emptiness will increase. As this happens, there is less and less need for analysis. At this point just look directly and then rest naturally. When distraction arises, look at that too. Everything can be used as an object of investigation in the practice of vipashyana. Look directly at distraction, drowsiness, agitation, or whatever arises and then relax naturally right within that freedom from fabrications.

The most effective way to practice this type of meditation is to alternate vipashyana with shamatha. Begin the session with resting meditation. When you are somewhat settled, you analyze. When analysis brings insight, rest in that. When you become unsettled, rest again, and so on.

When you become adept at this practice, you can leap. This is something that is beyond any technique. It involves letting original wisdom come to you. This is not a practice that can be explained, since it is completely beyond the conventional. The best way to get an understanding of this is to contemplate the teachings on buddha nature that we discussed in the previous chapter.

Whenever you practice meditation, it is good to begin the session by taking refuge in the Three Jewels. Appreciation for the teachers, teachings, and community are an antidote for smugness, which reinforces ego rather than exposing it. Make the aspiration to attain enlightenment for the benefit of all sentient beings. This is an antidote for self-centeredness. At the end of the session, dedicate whatever merit you have gained from the practice to the welfare of others. This is the precious motivation of the mahayana. Try not to be separated from it.

18

ACTION

EGO MASQUERADES AS SEER, doer, and adviser—seeking happiness and avoiding sorrow. Its real agenda is to keep the game going by churning out projections and reacting to them as though they were real. It continually provides the allure of desirable projections and the menace of undesirable ones. Hopes of possessing what we want and fears of getting what we don't want keep us spinning and avert the spotlight from ego's most basic deceit—our adviser is nothing but smoke and mirrors. Because we do not recognize the nature of these illusions, we circle in samsara, chasing chimeras and running from specters that are no more substantial than images in a dream.

The Buddha's prescription for undoing ego's deception is "the threefold training," which overcomes delusion and thoroughly reveals egolessness. The first part of the threefold training is developing the *prajna* that understands the view of egolessness. The second part—*samadhi*, or meditation—transforms this view into direct experience. The third part, *shila*—a Sanskrit term translated variously as "conduct," "discipline," "ethics," or "action"—shines the light of view and meditation into all the dark corners of our daily lives. The threefold training in prajna, samadhi, and shila is most effective when practiced as a unity. The main concern of this book has been prajna. In the previous chapter, we discussed samadhi. We conclude with a discussion of shila.

This is a vast topic, which we will touch on only briefly. It consists of the disciplines we engage in when we arise from listening, contemplating, and meditating. Shila is sometimes described as codes of conduct, or systems of ethical discipline or morality, but since it brings view and meditation into the activities of daily life, it is much more than this.

Ego's version of ethics is to practice virtue to get the best possible deal within samsara. This is better than nonvirtue, of course, but it is based on getting what we want and avoiding what we don't want. Therefore, it perpetuates samsara. The positive conditions produced by such virtue are temporary. When the positive states that come from this conduct wear out, unhappy conditions arise. The ethics that transcend samsara are virtues that are in harmony with genuine reality—egolessness—rather than ego's distorted perspective.

Often, these two approaches look similar. For example, both proscribe harming others. Ego's approach is to avoid harming others because you understand harming others will lead to your being harmed in the future. By not causing harm, you will definitely have a better time in samsara. Transcendent virtue also avoids harming others, but does so in order to overcome the egotism that places its interests above the well-being of others. Rather than striving for happiness in samsara, this approach aims to overcome the delusion and self-clinging that are samsara's root.

One way to understand shila is to look at how it is practiced in each of the three vehicles. The primary hinayana motivation is individual liberation, and the heart of the hinayana view is the selflessness of the individual. The conduct that accords with this motivation and view is called "the conduct of individual liberation." The discipline is to avoid causing harm to others as well as the thinking patterns that are the basis for causing harm. This is the foundation and common thread of all Buddhist approaches to conduct.

The conduct of individual liberation consists of abandoning ten types of unwholesome actions of body, speech, and mind:

- The three bodily negative actions are killing, taking what is not offered, and sexual misconduct.
- The four negative actions of speech are lying, slander, speaking harshly, and idle chatter.
- The three negative mental actions are envy, malice, and wrong views.

The actions of body and speech are the actual ways we harm others, while the actions of mind provide the motivation. All of these negative actions are based on self-clinging—the view of ego.

The mahayana approach to shila goes a step further. The heart of the mahayana view is twofold egolessness, which was discussed in chapter 15.* The motivation is the vast wish to free all beings from suffering, which arises from seeing the suffering others experience because they have not realized egolessness. Understanding that our capacity to liberate beings is limited by our own lack of realization, we vow to attain enlightenment for their benefit. This is the called "the bodhichitta aspiration." The conduct that accords with this view and motivation is called "bodhichitta discipline."

The bodhichitta discipline is the practice of the *paramitas*, or the "perfections," the transcendent actions of a bodhisattva. One way to translate the word *paramita* is "gone to the other shore." These actions transport us from the self-centered side of the river to the egoless side. The six paramitas are the practices of *generosity, ethics, patience, joyous diligence, meditation,* and *prajna.* These powerful methods go against ego's grain and undermine

---

* Pages 155–56.

self-centeredness, while directly helping others through action and example.

The *paramita of generosity* is the antidote to its opposite, clinging to "me" and "mine." Ego constantly finds things to hold on to: material objects, psychological comforts, and spiritual achievements. Generosity means letting go. The act of giving might involve letting go of physical possessions, but even more important is giving up pettiness and our struggle with the world. When generosity is free from focusing on the three spheres—the giver, the gift, and the recipient—it is the actual paramita of generosity.

The *paramita of ethics* is the antidote to the kleshas that cause the ten types of unwholesome action, described above. Relinquishing the kleshas, we engage in the opposite of the unwholesome actions, the ten wholesome actions. Instead of taking life, we try to protect it. Instead of stealing, we practice generosity, and so on. When ethics is free from focusing on the actor, the wholesome action, and the object of that action, it is the actual paramita of ethics.

The *paramita of patience* is the antidote to anger. It is based on compassion and prajna. The compassion aspect is seeing that the harm we experience from others comes from their suffering caused by the kleshas, ignorance, and confusion. The prajna aspect is seeing that the experiencer of the harm, the painful experience, and the cause of that pain have no self-nature. The patience that recognizes this is the actual paramita of patience.

The *paramita of joyous diligence* is the antidote to laziness and depression and the support for all the other paramitas. Laziness and depression are forms of self-clinging. Exertion comes from seeing selflessness, and therefore that we can step over laziness and depression, and cheer up unconditionally. Diligence is based on joy, not drudgery. When diligence is free from focusing on an actor, an action, and the object of that action, it is the actual paramita of joyous diligence.

The *paramita of meditation* is the antidote to wildness and distraction. Seeing that wildness and distraction are supports for ego's deceptions, we tame our mind and develop samadhi. When meditation is resting in the natural state, free from meditator, meditation technique, and object, it is the actual paramita of meditation.

The *paramita of prajna* is the antidote to delusion. It arises from listening, contemplating, and meditating. Prajna that knows genuine reality, just as it is, is the actual prajna paramita.

The vajrayana approach to shila is based on the view that wisdom primordially abides as the ground, covered over by temporary defilements. The motivation is to recognize this original purity and take it as the path. In harmony with this, vajrayana conduct is the "conduct of equality and purity": by recollecting again and again that all phenomena are equally the empty display of original wisdom, clinging to accepting and rejecting as truly real is abandoned. An example of vajrayana conduct is the practice of "pure perception," or "sacred outlook," where everything you see is regarded as the form of the deity, everything you hear is regarded as the sound of the deity's mantra, and everything you think is regarded as the deity's wisdom.

These different practices of shila are progressively more radical ways of going against our habitual patterns and exposing ego's duplicity. There are many variations on these disciplines, but the common element is boycotting or actively opposing ego's self-centered logic by acting in harmony with genuine reality.

The main point of shila is to learn to use ordinary life as the path, from drinking your morning tea or coffee to working with life's biggest challenges. You do this by joining daily activity with the view and meditation. Here, view means knowing that ego and its projections are delusions. Your trusty adviser is not looking after your interests at all, but keeping you bound in samsara. Meditation is learning to look directly at whatever happens and then resting with that. When situations get juicy, the instruction is to let ego cook in its own broth: look directly at the experience and then rest naturally without struggle. In this way you use the energy of ego to undermine ego, just as an aikido master uses the energy of an attacker to counter the attack.

Several years ago I had a challenging job that I loved and that was quite important to me. Things changed and I found myself working with a difficult person who seemed to be undermining everything I had accomplished. One day I went to lunch with a good friend and colleague and complained at length about my seemingly dysfunctional boss, the sorry state of affairs at work, my frustration and total lack of support. When I finished, my friend gently asked, "Isn't this a good time to practice what you have been teaching?"

The Buddha's first teaching was about the suffering that arises from not getting what you want, getting what you don't want, losing what you have, and from the simple realities of birth, old age, sickness, and death. He did not teach methods for avoiding them, but taught that the way to transcend suffering was to recognize their true nature and the true nature of the one who suffers. The real obstacles on the path are not the difficulties we will inevitably face but wanting things to be different. Because of this we do not see things as they are, and we are tormented by hopes and fears. As the *mahasiddha* Tilopa said to his student, Naropa, "Son, appearances don't bind you. It is attachment that binds you. So give up your attachment, Naropa!"

We need to learn how to take whatever we experience as the path: embarrassment is the path, disappointment is the path, confusion is the path. Of course this is not what we want to hear. We want to hear that if we practice well, we won't have to face such difficulties, and if things go wrong, the buddhas and gurus will protect us from such obstacles.

Once Trungpa Rinpoche was staying at Rocky Mountain Dharma Center, where he was approached by a young practitioner who was going on solitary retreat. She told him about the retreat and said that the only thing that worried her were the bears that had recently been spotted on the land. She asked if he could give her a mantra to protect her from bears. Trungpa Rinpoche responded, "You want a mantra to protect you from the bears? Of course. Come closer." The young lady moved closer to him. He gestured for her to come closer still. When she was right in front of his knees, he leaned down and whispered the mantra she was to recite: "They are coming to get me!"

This brings us to another key point. As long as there is ego, there will be irony. As long as there is irony, there are possibilities for humor. Ego-clinging is serious business. Humor is a great lubricant for our journey. A sense of humor is one of our most potent methods for overcoming ego-clinging. When you see yourself churning up the same delusive patterns again and again, it is easy to become frustrated and self-critical. However, feeling bad about yourself is another form of self-clinging. A sense of humor lets in fresh air to ventilate ego's stuffy seriousness. Ego's game is actually funny, but we are usually too wrapped up in it to notice.

One of the best ways to practice view, meditation, and conduct together is the mahayana practice of "the samadhi of illusion." This method is to recollect again and again that your experience is like a dream, like an illusion, like a movie, as you go about your daily life. You don't need to cling to this thought. Just use it to cut through your attachment to experience, and move on. Remind yourself that while things appear, they have no self-nature. There is a famous mind-training slogan that describes this practice: "Regard all dharmas as dreams."[1]

Since we constantly superimpose projections on appearances, and then react to our own projections, the samadhi of illusion is particularly useful when situations are painful or when strong kleshas arise. When you see someone you regard as an enemy, for example, look at them and recognize that "enemy" is your projection. The actual appearance is free from friend or enemy. The same thing is true for things you feel passion for, as well as the other objects of the kleshas, things you feel pride about, people you feel envious of, and so on. By recollecting again and again that appearances are free of whatever you imagine them to be, your clinging to things will gradually diminish and your experience will become more free-flowing.

CONCLUSION

In *Contemplating Reality*, we have looked at a series of profound views of reality. You may not be able to remember each one, but you can return to them again and again, and as you do, their power to undo ego's entanglements will increase (you can also refer to the table in appendix 2 for a quick refresher). While each view is more subtle than the views that preceded it, none of them is wrong. All have potency. I would like to end this book by discussing the way the practice of the samadhi of illusion can be adapted to whichever view you are working with.

If you are contemplating the Vaibhashika view, you can recollect that extended objects and durations of time appear but are not real; what actually exist are the briefest moments of consciousness and infinitesimal particles of matter. It is just thoughts that take them to be a self and objects. "Self" and "objects" are illusory.

If you are working with the Sautrantika view, recollect the difference between things that genuinely exist because they appear with their own specific characteristics and abstractions that do not actually exist that appear with general characteristics. The inconceivable and inexpressible sights, sounds, smells, and other phenomena that appear with specific characteristics are genuinely real. Concepts that appear with general characteristics do not truly exist. The visible form of your friend is genuine. Concepts about his or her goodness or badness, happiness or sadness, are not.

One way to work with the Chittamatra view is to recollect that there are no common appearances. A situation faced by a group of people will appear differently to each of them, even if everyone thinks they are looking at the same thing. Alternatively, remember that outer appearances are not truly existent—they are just mind's projections, like in a dream. Remember that the dualistic split between perceived and perceiver is dreamlike and illusory, and from time to time during the day, rest in nondual self-awareness for just a few moments.

To practice the samadhi of illusion with the Svatantrika view, periodically recall that all phenomena are not truly existent; they are illusory and dreamlike. You might also occasionally need to recollect a reason why this is so; for example, that phenomena have no inherent nature because they are neither one thing nor many things. From time to time, rest for a few moments in the true nature of reality, mere emptiness that is like space.

Working with the Prasangika view is similar to working with the Svatantrika view. To practice it, periodically recall that appearances are appearance-emptiness undifferentiable, like water-moons, reflections, and movies. When you can rest in meditative equipoise for a few moments, relax within the true nature of reality that is beyond all concepts about what it might be.

When practicing the samadhi of illusion with the Shentong view, recollect that the perfectly existent nature is nondual, original wisdom and all phenomena are wisdom's energy and play. They are like the rainbows that appear when you shine light through a crystal or like dreams when you know you are dreaming. From time to time, rest in great non-conceptual luminous clarity.

All of these methods involve recollecting the view of genuine reality in order to counteract our attachment to apparent reality. However you go about it, the samadhi of illusion is a good way to put these teachings into practice throughout your daily life.

By this virtue, may all beings complete the
   accumulations of merit and wisdom,
And may they attain the two genuine kayas
   that arise from merit and wisdom.

Acknowledgments

IT IS INCONCEIVABLY fortunate that the Lord Buddha appeared in this world, that his teachings continue to flourish, and that we have met with them in this life. It is said that the kindness of the Buddha is only exceeded by the kindness of one's own teachers, who make this meeting possible. There is no way to repay the kindness of my gurus. Whatever is of value in this book comes from them. I have merely tried to repeat the deep meaning they imparted using fresh words and examples. In particular, the Vidyadhara Chögyam Trungpa Rinpoche and Khenpo Tsültrim Gyamtso Rinpoche have been like fathers to me. May the light of their buddha activity spread throughout the world.

I am also very grateful to be able to study with The Dzogchen Ponlop Rinpoche, both at Nitartha Institute and elsewhere. His profundity, humor, and warmth transform the study of the great texts of the tradition from dry scholarship to living dharma. As the foremost student of Khenpo Rinpoche, Ponlop Rinpoche also demonstrates that the perfect teacher is a perfect student. I am particularly grateful that he contributed a foreword for this book.

I am very grateful for the teachings and life examples of Shunryu Suzuki Roshi, Ato Rinpoche, Dzongsar Khyentse Rinpoche, Yongey Mingyur Rinpoche, and Eido Shimano Roshi. We are all so fortunate that such accomplished masters have dedicated their lives to implanting the dharma in the West.

Many dharma brothers and sisters encouraged and assisted

me while I was writing this book. Barry Boyce, senior editor and staff writer of the *Shambhala Sun* and *Buddhadharma*, was the first to read each chapter. He suggested improvements with the precision of an acupuncturist, provided encouragement and sustenance for the long journey, and joined in lively and inspired discussions about the material that completely enriched the process and the result.

Larry Mermelstein, close friend and longtime director of the Nalanda Translation Committee, read the manuscript in its early stages, helped bring the project into focus, and provided support and wise counsel as the work progressed.

Scott Wellenbach, longtime colleague, mentor, and dear friend, patiently read the entire manuscript and pointed out inaccuracies and difficulties with the text, and suggested ways to improve them.

Another formidable translator and friend, Tyler Dewar, cheerfully read the entire manuscript and suggested numerous improvements.

Elizabeth Callahan, outstanding scholar-practitioner and friend, helped me clarify a number of difficult points during my research and was kind enough to let me read and quote from the manuscript of her important forthcoming *Treasury of Knowledge* volume, *Frameworks of Buddhist Philosophy*.

At the end of my work, the revision process was greatly enhanced by assistance from another good friend, Ari Goldfield, Khenpo Rinpoche's brilliant, devoted, and tireless secretary, who carefully read the manuscript and provided new translations from the Tibetan, extensive comments, and very insightful advice.

My dear friends Tim Olmsted, Jim Gimian, Melvin McLeod, Molly de Shong, Michael Speraw, Ani Tsultrim Palmo, and too many other people to mention, served as sounding boards, colleagues, and advisers. I am grateful for their good counsel and comradeship.

Carol Lamarche kindly prepared the index.

Emily Bower, my editor at Shambhala Publications, championed this book and guided me through the editorial and publishing processes with great kindness, grace, and skill.

Finally, I am grateful that my family has been completely supportive of these efforts. I offer heartfelt thanks to my mother, Madeline; my children, Alden and Missy, and Doug and Sierra; and especially my wife and companion, Wendy.

May there be benefit!

Halifax, Nova Scotia
April 13, 2006

Appendix 1

Biographical Sketches of the
Early Indian Masters

DETAILS OF THE LIFE stories of the early Buddhist masters are difficult to come by, and yet without a certain amount of background, it is hard to keep track of who's who, and who taught what. To help remedy this, here are a few short biographies. Much of this material is drawn from the *History of Buddhism in India*, a seventeenth-century text compiled by the renowned Tibetan master Jonang Taranatha.[1] It is supplemented with information from modern scholars.

When we investigate the lives of great Buddhist masters of the past, it is not easy to separate the mythic and hagiographic from the factual and historic. This is particularly true for Indian teachers, because much of the historical record was lost when "the Noble Land" was overrun by invaders during the twelfth and thirteenth centuries. Moreover, there is an interesting question about what actually is mythic and what actually is historic. For example, we believe that people live for a maximum of about one hundred years. When we are told that Nagarjuna lived for five hundred years, we conclude that that must be mythic. When we hear that Chandrakirti milked a painting of a cow, we conclude that also must be mythic. These conclusions merely follow the common consensus about what is real.

There is nothing wrong with following worldly consensus, but it is good to keep it in perspective. Khenpo Rinpoche has said that, "In order to believe in miracles, you must have the miraculous view." For example, once you understand that death does not truly exist; that death is like death in a dream; that time does not truly exist, and time is like time in a dream; then it seems plausible that someone who realizes the true nature of reality would be able to live for as long as they like. In a world where atoms do not truly exist and where everything is like a dream, what reason can we give to prove that a realized being would not be able to draw milk from the painting of a cow?

The following sketches touch on some of the most important teachers in the evolution of the teachings on the view. Some of them are mentioned in the main part of this book, but others are not. I have included the others here to give a fuller picture of the background of these teachings. Teachers are listed chronologically.

Nagarjuna (circa the second century). Very little is known about the life of Nagarjuna, the founder of the Madhyamaka system. He was probably born in southern India during the first or second century of the Common Era. Several sutras and tantras have passages that have been interpreted as predicting his life and teachings, including the *Lankavatara Sutra*, the *Great Cloud Sutra*, the *Great Drum Sutra*, and the *Manjushri Root Tantra*.

Traditional accounts say that Nagarjuna was born into a Brahmin family, became a Buddhist monk, went to the land of the *nagas* (water beings) to retrieve the *Prajna Paramita Sutra*, which had been kept there for protection, and composed many commentaries that clarified the meaning of the three turnings of the wheel of dharma. Writings attributed to him are traditionally classified into three collections: the *Collection of Advice*, which explains the way virtue and nonvirtue lead to nirvana and samsara respectively, as presented in the first turning of the wheel of dharma; the *Collection of Reasonings*, which focus on essence-lessness and comment on the *Prajnaparamita Sutras* from the middle turning of the wheel of dharma; and the *Collection of Praises*, which comment on the final turning of the wheel of dharma and focus on buddha nature. His most important text is the *Mulamadhyamakakarika*, or *The Fundamental Wisdom of the Middle Way*, which is from the *Collection of Reasonings*.

Aryadeva (circa the second century). Aryadeva was born in Sri Lanka, the son of a king. He abandoned his royal life to become a monk and study the dharma. While traveling in India on pilgrimage, he met Nagarjuna and became his foremost disciple. Together they are known as "the Father and Son," and also "the Madhyamikas of the Model Texts," since their texts form the foundation for all subsequent Middle Way teachings. Aryadeva's most important work is the *Catuhshataka*, or *The Four Hundred Verses*.

Aryadeva is also known as Kanadeva (One-eyed Deva) because while he was traveling to Nalanda University to engage a great Brahmin in debate, he encountered a *tirthika* (non-Buddhist or heretic) woman who asked for one of his eyes for a magical rite, which he gave to her. Upon arriving at Nalanda, he defeated the Brahmin and converted him, along with many of his followers, to the dharma.

Asanga (late fourth century to early fifth century). Asanga, the founder of the Yogachara system, was born in Purushapura in the region of Gandhara (now Peshawar in modern Pakistan). According to traditional accounts, he was Vasubandhu's older half brother or brother. Encouraged by his mother to devote his life to propagating the dharma, Asanga was ordained and devoted himself to practice and study. He had no difficulty learning the hinayana teachings and developing a general understanding of the mahayana, but found that the meaning of the Prajnaparamita Sutra completely eluded him.

To penetrate the profundity of the mahayana, he went on retreat in a cave in the mountains and meditated on Maitreya, the tenth-bhumi bodhisattva and regent of Shakyamuni Buddha. After three years of practicing, without even a sign in his dreams, Asanga became discouraged and left his retreat. As he was leaving, he saw a pigeon leaving its nest in the rock face and noticed how the entrance to the nest had been worn smooth by the feathers of generations of birds. Inspired by this example, he returned to his retreat. After three more years, Asanga again despaired, but this time as he was leaving his retreat he noticed stones that had been eroded by dripping water. Thinking that he needed to practice with more diligence, he returned to his retreat. After three more years, Asanga gave up hope and again left retreat. He came across a man who was rubbing an iron bar with a cotton cloth. When he asked the man what he was doing, the man replied that he was making a needle and showed Asanga a box of needles he had already made. Seeing how much diligence worldly people can have to achieve their goals, Asanga screwed up his courage and returned to retreat. After three more years, having spent a total of twelve years on retreat without a sign, he reached the depths of despair and left.

As he wandered along a dusty road, he came upon a dog with protruding ribs who was covered with maggot-infested sores. Overwhelmed by compassion, he thought that if he didn't remove the maggots, the dog would die, and if he did, the maggots would die. He cut a piece of flesh from his own thigh to place the maggots on. Fearing he might crush the maggots with his fingers as he tried to remove them from the starving dog, he closed his eyes and was about to remove the maggots with his tongue, but as he bent down his tongue touched the dusty ground. Looking up, he beheld Maitreya face-to-face. Asanga demanded to know where Maitreya had been while he had struggled to see him for twelve long years. Maitreya responded that they had never been separate, but that Asanga's obscurations had prevented him from recognizing that.

After this, Maitreya brought Asanga to his pure land and extensively taught him the mahayana, including the texts that later became known as the *Five Treatises of Maitreya*: the *Abhisamayalankara*, or *The Ornament of Clear Realization*; the *Mahayanasutralankara*, or *The Ornament of the Mahayana Sutras*; the *Dharma-dharmata-vibhanga*, or *Distinguishing Phenomena from Pure Being*; the *Madhyantavibhanga* or *Distinguishing the Middle from the Extremes*; and the *Mahayanottaratantrashastra*, or *The Treatise on Buddha Nature* (also known as the *Ratnagotra-vibhaga*). In addition to writing down these texts, Asanga composed a number of important commentaries of his own, including the *Abhidharmasamuchchaya*, or *The Compendium of Abhidharma*; the *Mahayana-samgraha*, or *The Compendium of the Mahayana*; and the *Yogachara-bhumi*, or *The Bhumis of Yogic Practice*.

Vasubandhu (late fourth century to mid fifth century). Vasubandhu, like his older brother, Asanga, was born in Purusapura in Gandhara and was encouraged by their mother to become a monk and devote himself to the dharma. Initially, he studied the Vaibhashika system, but when doubts about it arose, he went on to study Sautrantika. Later, to clarify his understanding of these two systems, he spent four years studying in Kashmir, the center of "orthodox" Vaibhashika learning.

Returning to Gandhara, he supported himself by teaching the dharma to the public. At the end of each day, he composed a summary verse for the day's teachings, and in this way composed more than six hundred verses, which became the *Abhidharmakosha*, or *The Treasury of Abhidharma*, which is widely regarded as the definitive text on the Vaibhashika system. He subsequently wrote an auto-commentary on the *Kosha* that criticizes the Vaibhashika teachings from a Sautrantika point of view.

It is said that Vasubandhu had little respect for the mahayana teachings and did not consider them the teachings of the Buddha. He is quoted disparaging his brother's *Bhumis of Yogic Practice* and the Yogachara system in general. That was to change, and there are several versions of the story of Vasubandhu's conversion to the mahayana. In one, Asanga sent two students to Vasubandhu who recited sutras that convinced him of the validity of the mahayana view and practice. In another, Asanga pretended to be seriously ill, and when Vasubandhu visited him, explained the mahayana to him, convincing him of its superiority.

After his conversion, Vasubandhu was deeply embarrassed about having deprecated the mahayana and was about to cut out his own tongue, when Asanga told him that the way to atone for his behavior was to propagate the mahayana doctrine widely. Vasubandhu composed many important Yogachara texts, including the *Vimshatika*, or *The Twenty Verses*; the *Trimshika-karika*, or *The Thirty Verses*; the *Trisvabhava-nirdesha*, or *The Treatise on the Three Natures*; as well as commentaries on three of the five treatises of Maitreya: *The Ornament of the Mahayana Sutras*, *Distinguishing Phenomena from Pure Being*, and *Distinguishing the Middle from the Extremes*.

Dignaga (late fifth to mid sixth century). Dignaga, founder of the Buddhist epistemological tradition, was born to a Brahmin family near Kanchi, in southern India, not far from modern Bangalore. He first studied in the hinayana Vatsiputriya school, but was not satisfied with these teachings. Later he studied the Yogachara system at Nalanda. Some sources say that he studied with Vasubandhu, but modern scholars find this unlikely. After leaving Nalanda, Dignaga returned to the south and retired to a cave to practice meditation and write commentaries on Yogachara and logic.

Although Nagarjuna, Vasubandhu, and others had discussed sources and types of knowledge and logic, Dignaga was the first person to articulate a comprehensive Buddhist system of *pramana*, or the means of valid cognition, in his *Pramanasamuchchaya*, or *The Compendium on Valid Cognition*.

Buddhapalita (circa sixth century). Buddhapalita was born in Hamsakrida, in Tambala, southern India. He wrote commentaries on the works of Nagarjuna and Aryadeva, and is best known for composing one of the first commentaries on *The Fundamental Wisdom of the Middle Way* (referred to simply as the *Buddhapalita*) in which he mainly used Nagarjuna's Consequentialist method of reasoning, not making assertions of his own but using logical reasoning to demonstrate the illogical consequences *(prasanga)* of the views of others. His commentary was later strongly criticized by Bhavaviveka, and then defended by Chandrakirti. This controversy marked the division of Nagarjuna's tradition into the Svatantrika, or Autonomy school, and the Prasangika, or Consequence school (see below).

Bhavaviveka (circa sixth century). Bhavaviveka, also referred to as Bhavya, was born in Malyara, in southern India. His interests included both the Madhyamaka teachings of Nagarjuna and Aryadeva and the logical tradition of Dignaga. He was the first person to apply Dignaga's logical methods to Madhyamaka in his commentary on *The Fundamental Wisdom of the Middle Way*, called the *Prajna-pradipa*, or *The Lamp of Prajna*. In this work, he criticized Buddhapalita for failing to use Autonomous reasonings *(svatantra)* and examples to refute opponents of the Middle Way.

Chandrakirti (sixth to seventh century). Chandrakirti, regarded by others as the founder of the Middle Way Consequence school, was born in Samanta (or Samana), in southern India, and became abbot of Nalanda University. He composed two important commentaries on *The Fundamental Wisdom of the Middle Way*. The first, the *Madhyamakavatara*, or *The Entrance to the Middle Way*, is a commentary on the general meaning of Nagarjuna's text. It provides an accessible and gradual introduction to topics that are cryptic and difficult to understand in the original. While it seems not to have been widely studied during Chandrakirti's lifetime, in Tibet the *Madhyamakavatara* eventually became the principal text used to introduce students to the Middle Way teachings.

The second commentary is the *Prasannapada*, or *The Lucid Words*, a much more detailed commentary on *The Fundamental Wisdom of the Middle Way*. This latter work includes an extensive criticism of Bhavaviveka's use of Autonomous reasonings and defends Buddhapalita's work.

Not only was Chandrakirti a great scholar, he was also a renowned *siddha* (accomplished master). Once Chandrakirti was walking through the halls of Nalanda and bumped into a stone pillar. One of his students said, "What about your emptiness now!" In reply, Chandrakirti passed his hand through the pillar. Another time, Chandrakirti was in charge of Nalanda's food stores when there was a famine in the region. It is said that he drew a picture of a cow on the wall, and milked it, thus providing food for the sangha and reversing everyone's clinging to true existence. Another time, when an invading army was approaching the university, Chandrakirti made the stone lions at Nalanda's gates rise up and roar, scaring away the invaders and bringing peace to the land.

Dharmakirti (circa seventh century). Dharmakirti was born to a Brahmin family in the southern kingdom of Chudamani. At first he studied the Vedas and the traditional arts and sciences, but his education was disrupted when he came upon some Buddhist texts and found them convincing. Leaving his community to study the dharma, he eventually arrived at Nalanda, where he studied under Ishvarasena, a disciple of Dignaga (some accounts say it was Dharmapala, another of Dignaga's disciples). It is said that the first time Ishvarasena expounded Dignaga's *Pramanasamuchchaya*, Dharmakirti understood the text as well as his teacher. After clarifying certain points, he asked Ishvarasena to explain the text again. This time, his understanding was equal to Dignaga's. Upon hearing it presented a third time, it is said that Dharmakirti understood the implications of Dignaga's work, and saw the shortcoming of Ishvarasena's understanding. Ishvarasena declared that Dharmakirti had become the equal to Dignaga and had him write a commentary on the text.

Dharmakirti composed seven treatises on valid cognition, the most important of which is the *Pramanavarttika*, or *The Commentary on Valid Cognition*.

Shantideva (eighth century). Shantideva, author of the *Bodhicharyavatara*, or *The Way of the Bodhisattva*, was born a prince in Surashtra (now Surat in Gujarat State in India). When he was about to be enthroned as king, he dreamed that Manjushri and Tara warned him not to ascend the throne. Leaving the kingdom, he meditated in the wilderness and had many visions of Manjushri. Eventually he traveled to Nalanda, where he took ordination and studied the sutras and tantras. It is said that during this period he secretly wrote two important works, the *Shikshasamuchchaya*, or *The Compendium of Teachings*, and the *Sutrasamuchchaya*, or *The Compendium of Sutras* (which has since been lost), but to all outward appearances, all he did was eat, sleep, and shit.

His fellow scholars thought that Shantideva was a complete deadbeat, and decided to shame him into leaving the university. They organized a rotation of sutra recitation, but when Shantideva's turn came, he demurred. On being pressed, he said that if they prepared a teaching throne for him, he would take a turn. This was done, and the scholars assembled to see him humiliated. Shantideva ascended the lion throne and asked the assembly if they wanted to hear existing teachings or something new. Everyone said to recite something new. He then recited the *Bodhicharyavatara*. When he reached the ninth chapter, on the topic of prajna, he rose up into the air and disappeared from sight, but his voice continued to be heard as he finished the text.

The scholars recorded different versions of the scripture, and could not agree which was most authentic. When they learned that Shantideva was living in a city called Kalinga, three representatives were sent to invite him to return to Nalanda. Shantideva declined, but did tell them which version of the *Bodhicharyavatara* was accurate, and where they could find the *Shikshasamuchchaya* and the *Sutrasamuchchaya*.

The *Bodhicharyavatara* has become one of the most widely studied, practiced, and revered Buddhist treatises, both for its penetrating instructions in mahayana conduct and for its profound presentation of the Prasangika view.

Shanta-rakshita (eighth century). Shanta-rakshita, also known as Acharya Bodhisattva and Khenpo Bodhisattva, was born in eastern Bengal, the son of the king of Zahor. Little is known about his early life, but he became the abbot of Nalanda and later traveled to Tibet at the invitation of King Trisong Detsen. In Tibet he established the first major Buddhist institutions and began the construction of Samye Monastery. When negative forces disrupted the project, he advised the king to invite Guru Padmasambhava to Tibet to subdue them. He instructed and ordained the first seven monks in Tibet and initiated a major program of translating the dharma.

Shanta-rakshita's most important writings are the *Madhyamakalankara*, or *The Ornament of the Middle Way*, and the *Tattvasamgraha*, or *The Compendium of Suchness*. As a scholar, he achieved an important synthesis of diverse streams of the mahayana by bringing together the teachings of the Middle Way,

Mind Only, and valid cognition, creating a coherent and consistent system. This Yogachara-Madhyamaka synthesis was the last great development of the view teachings in India. Shantarakshita's work was carried on by Kamalashila, his main Indian disciple.

The Two Charioteers, the Six Ornaments of the World, the Six Great Charioteers, and so on. Many epithets are used to refer to these masters. Nagarjuna and Asanga are sometimes called the "Two Charioteers" because they were the founders of the two main mahayana traditions: the Madhyamaka, or the lineage of profound view, and the Yogachara, or the lineage of vast action.

Six of these masters—Nagarjuna, Aryadeva, Asanga, Vasubandhu, Dignaga, and Dharmakirti—are referred to as "the Six Ornaments of the World" or "Six Great Charioteers" because of their profound role in shaping the mahayana tradition.

Nalanda University. Nalanda University, or Nalanda Mahavihara, flourished for hundreds of years as one of the greatest centers of learning in the world. It was not purely a Buddhist institution but included teachers from many traditions who studied together and engaged in open debate. Almost all of the Indian masters mentioned here either trained, participated in great debates, or were abbots at Nalanda. At its peak, over 10,000 students and 1,500 teachers studied there.

In 1193, the university was destroyed by Muslim invaders. This was one of the final milestones in the disappearance of Buddhism in India. The ruins of Nalanda are located southeast of modern Patna, in Bihar State, India.

Appendix 2

The Stages of Meditation on Emptiness

Based on *The Treasury of Knowledge.*

	APPARENT REALITY (the way things appear)	GENUINE REALITY (the way things really are)
1st stage: Vaibhashika or Particularist school	Coarse objects	Most minute particles of matter and most subtle moments of consciousness
2nd stage: Sautrantika or Sutra school	Concepts and things that cannot perform a function	What is directly perceived and things that can perform a function

	APPARENT REALITY (the way things appear)	GENUINE REALITY (the way things really are)
3rd stage: Chittamatra or Mind Only school	Dependently arisen appearances imagined to be objects and subjects	Consciousness, free from the duality of perceiving subjects and perceived objects
Madhyamaka or Middle Way schools		
• Rangtong or Self-Empty schools		
— 4th stage: Svatantrika or Autonomy school	Illusionlike phenomena	Emptiness like space
— 5th stage: Prasangika or Consequence school	Whatever ordinary people believe truly exist	Free from complexity and beyond all thought and expression
• 6th stage: Shentong or Empty-of-Other school	Dependently arisen appearances imagined to be objects and subjects	Original wisdom, inseparable clarity/ emptiness

Notes

CHAPTER ONE

1. Dharmakirti, trans. Ari Goldfield. Personal communication.

2. Khenpo Tsültrim Gyamtso, *Ascertaining Certainty About the View: Chapter Seven, Section Three, from The Treasury of Knowledge by Jamgön Kongtrul Lodrö Thayé*, trans. and ed. Michele Martin (Auckland, N.Z.: Zhyisil Chokyi Ghatsal, 2001), 19.

3. Ibid., 26–27.

4. Ibid., 101.

5. Patrul Rinpoche, *The Words of My Perfect Teacher*, trans. Padmakara Translation Group, 2nd ed. (Boston: Shambhala, 1998), 252.

6. Jamgön Kongtrul Lodrö Thayé, *Creation and Completion: Essential Points of Tantric Meditation*, trans. and annotated by Sarah Harding (Boston: Wisdom, 2002), 30–31.

CHAPTER TWO

1. Khenpo Tsültrim Gyamtso, *Ascertaining Certainty*, 100.

2. Shunryu Suzuki, *Zen Mind, Beginner's Mind* (New York: Walker/Weatherhill, 1971), 46.

3. *The Sutra of the Heart of Transcendent Knowledge*, trans. Nalanda Translation Committee (Halifax, N.S.: Nalanda Translation Committee).

4. Arya Maitreya, Jamgön Kongtrul Lodrö Thayé, and Khenpo Tsültrim Gyamtso, *Buddha Nature: The Mahayana Uttaratantra-*

shastra with Commentary, trans. Rosemarie Fuchs (Ithaca, N.Y.: Snow Lion, 2000), 23.

CHAPTER THREE

1. Patrul Rinpoche, *Words of My Perfect Teacher*, 251.

CHAPTER FOUR

1. Milarepa, *Stories and Songs of Milarepa*, trans. Ari Goldfield (Halifax, N.S.: Marpa Translation Committee, 2003), 13.

2. Nawang Gehlek, *Good Life, Good Death: Tibetan Wisdom on Reincarnation* (New York: Riverhead Books, 2001), 101–102.

3. Shantideva, *The Way of the Bodhisattva: A Translation of the Bodhicharyavatara*, trans. Padmakara Translation Group (Boston: Shambhala, 1997), 82.

4. Francis Crick, *The Astonishing Hypothesis: The Scientific Search for the Soul* (New York: Scribner, 1994), 3.

5. Chögyam Trungpa, *Transcending Madness: The Experience of the Six Bardos* (Boston: Shambhala, 1992), 28–29.

6. Chandrakirti, "*Entering the Middle Way*," trans. Ari Goldfield (unpublished manuscript), 1:3.

CHAPTER FIVE

1. Quoted in Dzogchen Ponlop and Tenpa Gyaltsen, *The Gateway That Reveals the Philosophical Systems to Fresh Minds: An Exposition That Reveals the Presentation of the Philosophical Systems of Our Own Buddhist Faction in a Slightly Elaborate Way*, trans. Karl Brunnhölzl (Halifax, N.S.: Nitartha Institute, 2001), 8.

2. Chögyam Trungpa, *The Heart of the Buddha* (Boston: Shambhala, 1991), 43.

3. Chögyam Trungpa, *Cutting Through Spiritual Materialism* (Berkeley, Calif.: Shambhala, 1973), 8.

4. Mipham Gyamtso, *Gateway to Knowledge: The Treatise Entitled*

the Gate for Entering the Way of a Pandita, vol. 1, trans. Erik Pema Kunsang (Hong Kong: Rangjung Yeshe, 1997), 34.

5. Ibid., 30.

6. Khenpo Tsültrim Gyamtso, *The Sun of Wisdom: Teachings on the Noble Nagarjuna's Fundamental Wisdom of the Middle Way*, trans. Ari Goldfield (Boston: Shambhala, 2003), 114.

7. Khenchen Kunzang Palden, *Wisdom: Two Buddhist Commentaries on the Ninth Chapter of Shantidevas's* Bodhicharyavatara, ed. Khenchen Kunzang Palden, trans. Padmakara Translation Group (Peyzac-le-Moustier, France: Editions Padmakara, 1993), 25.

CHAPTER SIX

1. The Dzogchen Ponlop Rinpoche, *Lorik: Oral Commentary* (Halifax, N.S.: Nitartha Institute, 1996), 259.

2. Adapted from Khenpo Tsültrim Gyamtso, *Mahamudra Vipashyana*, trans. Jules B. Levinson, Michele Martin, and Jim Scott (Halifax, N.S.: Vajravairochana Translation Committee, 1993), 123.

3. Quoted in Ponlop and Gyaltsen, *Gateway That Reveals the Philosophical Systems*, 24.

A POETIC INTERLUDE

1. Chögyam Trungpa, *Dharma Art* (Boston: Shambhala, 1996), 115.

2. Matsuo Bashō, Yosa Buson, and Kobayashi Issa, *The Essential Haiku: Versions of Bashō, Buson, and Issa*, trans. and ed. Robert Hass (Hopewell, N.J.: Ecco Press, 1994), 23, 35, 37, 39, 53.

3. Ibid., 89, 112, 124.

4. Ibid., 161, 173, 186.

CHAPTER SEVEN

1. S. W. Hawking, *A Brief History of Time: From the Big Bang to Black Holes* (Toronto, and New York: Bantam Books, 1988), 2.

2. Public Broadcasting System, "The Elegant Universe: String's the Thing" (2003), www.pbs.org/wgbh/nova/elegant/view-gross.html.

3. "Facing Up to the Problem of Consciousness," *Journal of Consciousness Studies* 2, no. 3 (1995).

4. Tendzin Gyamtso Dalai Lama XIV and Howard C. Cutler, *The Art of Happiness: A Handbook for Living* (New York: Riverhead Books, 1998), 5–7.

5. The Dzogchen Ponlop Rinpoche, "A Science of Mind" (2003), www.nalandabodhi.org/science_of_mind.html.

6. *Songs of Realization*, trans. Marpa Translation Committee (Ashland, Ore.: Marpa Translation Committee, 2002), 3.

CHAPTER EIGHT

1. Jamgön Kongtrul Lodrö Thayé, *The Treasury of Knowledge*, trans. Ari Goldfield. Personal communication.

2. Quoted in Karmapa Wangchuk Dorje, *Mahamudra: The Ocean of Definitive Meaning*, trans. Elizabeth M. Callahan (Seattle: Nitartha International, 2001), 160.

3. Quoted in Jamgön Kongtrul Lodrö Thayé, *Gaining Certainty About the Provisional and the Definitive Meanings in the Three Turnings of the Wheel of Dharma, the Two Truths, and Dependent Arising: The Root Text and Commentary, Section Two of Chapter Seven from* The Treasury of Knowledge, trans. Anne Burchardi and Ari Goldfield (Kathmandu: Marpa Institute, 1997), 70.

4. Chögyam Trungpa, *Transcending Madness*, 28–29.

5. Quoted in Thrangu Rinpoche, *Distinguishing Dharma and Dharmata by Asanga and Maitreya, with a Commentary by Thrangu Rinpoche Geshe Lharamapa*, trans. Jules B. Levinson (Boulder: Namo Buddha Seminar, 1999), 15.

6. Maitreyanatha, Khenpo Tsültrim Gyamtso, and Mipham Gyamtso, *Maitreya's Distinguishing Phenomena and Pure Being*, trans. Jim Scott (Ithaca, N.Y.: Snow Lion, 2004), 99–101.

7. Ibid., 97.

8. Mipham Gyamtso, trans. Ari Goldfield, personal communication.

9. Jamgön Kongtrul Lodrö Thayé, "Frameworks of Buddhist Philosophy, Book Six: Part Three, a Systematic Presentation of the Cause-Based Philosophical Vehicles," trans. Elizabeth M. Callahan (forthcoming publication from Snow Lion), 76.

10. Quoted in Karmapa Wangchuk Dorje, *Ocean of Definitive Meaning*, 160.

11. Quoted in Khenpo Tsültrim Gyamtso, *The Gradual Path of the Heart of Wisdom*, trans. Elizabeth M. Callahan, Jules B. Levinson, and Michele Martin (Halifax, N.S.: Vajravairochana Translation Committee, 1995), 49.

12. Patrul Rinpoche, *Words of My Perfect Teacher*, 56.

13. Ibid., 57.

14. Shanta-rakshita and Mipham Gyamtso, *The Adornment of the Middle Way: Shanta-rakshita's Madhyamakalankara with Commentary by Jamgon Mipham*, trans. Padmakara Translation Group (Boston: Shambhala, 2005), 125.

CHAPTER NINE

1. Thrangu Rinpoche, *Distinguishing the Middle from the Extremes by Asanga and Maitreya: A Commentary by Thrangu Rinpoche Geshe Lharamapa*, trans. Jules B. Levinson (Boulder: Namo Buddha Seminar, 2000), 15.

2. Jamgön Kongtrul Lodrö Thayé, "Frameworks of Buddhist Philosophy," 71.

CHAPTER TEN

1. Khenpo Tsültrim Gyamtso, *The Sun of Wisdom*, 96.

2. Ibid., 42.

3. Ibid., 95.

4. Ibid., 181.

5. Suzuki, *Zen Mind*, 104.

6. Shanta-rakshita and Mipham Gyamtso, *Adornment of the Middle Way*, 121–22.

7. Ibid., 120–21.

8. Maitreyanatha, Khenpo Tsültrim Gyamtso, and Mipham Gyamtso, *Distinguishing Phenomena*, 109.

ANOTHER INTERLUDE

1. Used with the kind permission of Python (Monty) Pictures Ltd.

CHAPTER ELEVEN

1. *The Heart Sutra*, 1–2.
2. Khenpo Tsültrim Gyamtso, *Sun of Wisdom*, 119.
3. Shantideva, *Way of the Bodhisattva*, 137.
4. Shanta-rakshita and Mipham Gyamtso, *Adornment of the Middle Way*, 125–27.
5. Jamgön Kongtrul Lodrö Thayé, "Frameworks of Buddhist Philosophy," 92–93.
6. Ibid., 114.
7. Jamgön Kongtrul Lodrö Thayé, *The Treasury of Knowledge*, trans. Ari Goldfield, personal communication.
8. Ibid.

CHAPTER TWELVE

1. Longchen Yeshe Dorje, *Treasury of Precious Qualities: A Commentary on the Root Text of Jigme Lingpa Entitled the Quintessence of the Three Paths*, trans. Padmakara Translation Group (Boston: Shambhala, 2001), 337.
2. Jamgön Kongtrul Lodrö Thayé, "Frameworks of Buddhist Philosophy," 103.

CHAPTER THIRTEEN

1. Thrangu Rinpoche, *The Open Door to Emptiness*, trans. Shakya Dorje (Boulder: Namo Buddha, 1997), 52.
2. Khenpo Tsültrim Gyamtso, *The Sun of Wisdom*, 5.

3. Chandrakirti, *Entering the Middle Way*, 6:104ab.
4. *Songs of Realization*, 91.

CHAPTER FOURTEEN

1. Khenpo Tsültrim Gyamtso, *The Sun of Wisdom*, 66.
2. Chandrakirti, *Entering the Middle Way*, 6:37–38ab.
3. Khenpo Tsültrim Gyamtso, *The Sun of Wisdom*, 156.
4. Ibid., 157.
5. Milarepa, *Stories and Songs of Milarepa*, 12.

CHAPTER FIFTEEN

1. Chandrakirti, *Entering the Middle Way*, 6:20.
2. Ibid., 6:124ab.
3. Ibid., 6:127ab.
4. Ibid., 6:129abc.
5. Ibid., 6:147.
6. Ibid., 6:138–39.
7. Ibid., 6:145.
8. Ibid., 6:151–65.

CHAPTER SIXTEEN

1. Khenpo Tsültrim Gyamtso, *Progressive Stages of Meditation on Emptiness*, trans. and arranged by Shenpen Hookham, Prajna Editions (Auckland, N.Z: Zhyisil Chokyi Ghatsal, 2001), 79.
2. Maitreya, Jamgön Kongtrul Lodrö Thayé, and Khenpo Tsültrim Gyamtso, *Buddha Nature*, 34–35
3. Ibid., 23.
4. Ibid., 25.
5. Ibid., 26.
6. Ibid., 26.
7. Ibid., 27.
8. Ibid., 47.

9. Jamgön Kongtrul Lodrö Thayé, "Frameworks of Buddhist Philosophy," 122–23.

10. Maitreya and Mipham Gyamtso, "The Ornament of the Mahayana Sutras by Maitreya, chap, 7: 'Suchness,' with Commentary from A Feast of Nectar," trans. Elizabeth M. Callahan (unpublished manuscript), 16–17.

11. Jamgön Kongtrul Lodrö Thayé, The Treasury of Knowledge, trans. Ari Goldfield, personal communication.

12. Jamgön Kongtrul Lodrö Thayé, "Frameworks of Buddhist Philosophy," 124.

13. Ibid., 125.

14. Quoted in Karl Brunnhölzl, The Center of the Sunlit Sky: Madhyamaka in the Kagyü Tradition: Including a Translation of Pawo Rinpoche's Commentary on the Knowledge Section of Shantideva's the Entrance to the Bodhisattva's Way of Life (Bodhicaryavatara) (Ithaca, N.Y.: Snow Lion, 2004), 522.

15. Khenpo Tsültrim Gyamtso, Ascertaining Certainty, 192.

LAST INTERLUDE

1. Songs of Realization, 104.

CHAPTER EIGHTEEN

1. Chögyam Trungpa, Training the Mind & Cultivating Loving-Kindness (Boston: Shambhala, 1993), 29.

APPENDIX ONE

1. Taranatha's History of Buddhism in India, trans. Lama Chimpa and Alaka Chattopadhyaya, and ed. Debiprasad Chattopadhyaya (Delhi: Motilal Banarsidass, 1990).

Bibliography

Bashō Matsuo, Yosa Buson, and Kobayashi Issa. *The Essential Haiku: Versions of Bashō, Buson, and Issa.* Translated and edited by Robert Hass. Hopewell, N.J.: Ecco Press, 1994.

Brunnhölzl, Karl. *The Center of the Sunlit Sky: Madhyamaka in the Kagyü Tradition, Including a Translation of Pawo Rinpoche's Commentary on the Knowledge Section of Shantideva's the Entrance to the Bodhisattva's Way of Life* (Bodhicaryavatara). Ithaca, N.Y: Snow Lion Publications, 2004.

Chalmers, David John. *Facing up to the Problem of Consciousness.* Vol. 2, no. 3. Charlottesville, Va.: Journal of Consciousness Studies, 1995.

Chandrakirti. "Entering the Middle Way." Translated by Ari Goldfield: Unpublished manuscript.

Crick, Francis. *The Astonishing Hypothesis: The Scientific Search for the Soul.* New York: Scribner, 1994.

Dorje, Karmapa Wangchuk. *Mahamudra: The Ocean of Definitive Meaning.* Translated by Elizabeth M. Callahan. Seattle, Wash.: Nitartha International, 2001.

Gehlek, Nawang. *Good Life, Good Death: Tibetan Wisdom on Reincarnation.* New York: Riverhead Books, 2001.

Gyamtso, Khenpo Tsültrim. *Ascertaining Certainty About the View: Chapter Seven, Section Three from the Treasury of Knowledge by Jamgön Kongtrul Lodrö Thaye.* Translated by and edited by Michele Martin. Auckland, New Zealand: Zhyisil Chokyi Ghatsal Publications, 2001.

———. *The Gradual Path of the Heart of Wisdom.* Translated by Elizabeth M. Callahan, Jules B. Levinson and Michele Martin. Halifax, Nova Scotia: Vajravairochana Translation Committee, 1995.

———. *Mahamudra Vipashyana*. Translated by Jules B. Levinson, Michele Martin, and Jim Scott. Halifax, Nova Scotia: Vajravairochana Translation Committee, 1993.

———. *A Presentation of the Two Truths in the Three Yanas and the Mahayana Philosophical Traditions: A Seminar Given at Rocky Mountain Dharma Center Summer 1991*. Translated by Jules B. Levinson, Michele Martin, and Jim Scott. Halifax, Nova Scotia: Nalanda Translation Committee, 1992.

———. *Progressive Stages of Meditation on Emptiness*. Translated by and arranged by Shenpen Hookham. Vol. Prajna Editions. Auckland, N.Z: Zhyisil Chokyi Ghatsal Publications, 2001.

———. *The Sun of Wisdom: Teachings on the Noble Nagarjuna's Fundamental Wisdom of the Middle Way*. Translated by Ari Goldfield. Boston: Shambhala Publications, 2003.

———. *The Two Truths*. Translated by Ari Goldfield. Auckland, New Zealand: Zhyisil Chokyi Ghatsal Publications, 2001.

Gyamtso, Mipham. *Gateway to Knowledge: The Treatise Entitled the Gate for Entering the Way of a Pandita*. Vol. 1. Translated by Erik Pema Kunsang. Hong Kong: Rangjung Yeshe Publications, 1997.

Hawking, S. W. *A Brief History of Time: From the Big Bang to Black Holes*. New York: Bantam Books, 1988.

Kongtrul Lodrö Thaye. *Creation & Completion: Essential Points of Tantric Meditation*. Translated by and annotated by Sarah Harding. Boston: Wisdom Publications, 2002.

———. *Frameworks of Buddhist Philosophy: The Causal Vehicles, Book Six, Part Three, a Systematic Presentation of the Cause Based Philosophical Vehicles*. Translated by Elizabeth M. Callahan. Ithaca, N.Y.: Snow Lion Publications, (forthcoming).

———. *Gaining Certainty About the Provisional and the Definitive Meanings in the Three Turnings of the Wheel of Dharma, the Two Truths, and Dependent Arising: The Root Text and Commentary, Section Two of Chapter Seven from the Treasury of Knowledge*. Translated by Anne Burchardi and Ari Goldfield. Kathmandu, Nepal: Marpa Institute, 1997.

Longchen Yeshe Dorje. *Treasury of Precious Qualities: A Commentary on the Root Text of Jigme Lingpa Entitled the Quintessence of the Three Paths.* Translated by Padmakara Translation Group. Boston: Shambhala Publications, 2001.

Maitreya, and Mipham Gyamtso. "The Ornament of the Mahayana Sutras by Maitreya, Chapter Seven: Suchness: With Commentary from a Feast of Nectar." Translated by Elizabeth M. Callahan. Unpublished manuscript.

Maitreya, Arya, Kongtrul Lodrö Thaye, and Khenpo Tsültrim Gyamtso. *Buddha Nature: The Mahayana Uttaratantra Shastra with Commentary.* Translated by Rosemarie Fuchs. Ithaca, N.Y.: Snow Lion Publications, 2000.

Maitreyanatha, Khenpo Tsültrim Gyamtso, and Mipham Gyamtso. *Maitreya's Distinguishing Phenomena and Pure Being.* Translated by Jim Scott. Ithaca, N.Y.: Snow Lion Publications, 2004.

Milarepa. *Stories and Songs of Milarepa.* Translated by Ari Goldfield. Halifax, Nova Scotia: Marpa Translation Committee, 2003.

Palden, Khenchen Kunzang. *Wisdom: Two Buddhist Commentaries on the Ninth Chapter of Shantidevas's Bodhicharyavatara.* Translated by Padmakara Translation Group. Edited by Kunzang Palden Khenchen. Peyzac-le-Moustier, France: Editions Padmakara, 1993.

Patrul Rinpoche. *The Words of My Perfect Teacher.* Translated by the Padmakara Translation Group. 2nd ed. Boston: Shambhala Publications, 1998.

Ponlop, Dzogchen. *Lorik: Oral Commentary.* Halifax, Nova Scotia: Nitartha Institute, 1996.

———. A Science of Mind, 2003.

Ponlop, Dzogchen, and Tenpa Gyaltsen. *The Gateway That Reveals the Philosophical Systems to Fresh Minds: An Exposition That Reveals the Presentation of the Philosophical Systems of Our Own Buddhist Faction in a Slightly Elaborate Way.* Translated by Karl Brunnhölzl. Halifax, Nova Scotia: Nitartha Institute, 2001.

Shantarakshita, and Mipham Gyamtso. *The Adornment of the Middle Way: Shantarakshita's Madhyamakalankara with Commentary by*

Jamgon Mipham. Translated by Padmakara Translation Group. 1st ed. Boston: Shambhala Publications, 2005.

Shantideva. *The Way of the Bodhisattva: A Translation of the Bodhicharyavatara.* Translated by the Padmakara Translation Group. Boston: Shambhala Publications, 1997.

Songs of Realization. Translated by Marpa Translation Committee. Ashland, Ore.: Marpa Translation Committee, 2002.

Suzuki, Shunryu. *Zen Mind, Beginner's Mind.* New York: Weatherhill, 1971.

Taranatha, Jonang. *Taranatha's History of Buddhism in India.* Translated by Lama Chimpa and Alaka Chattopadhyaya. Edited by Debiprasad Chattopadhyaya. Delhi: Motilal Banarsidass, 1990.

Tendzin Gyamtso Dalai Lama XIV, and Howard C. Cutler. *The Art of Happiness: A Handbook for Living.* New York: Riverhead Books, 1998.

The Sutra of the Heart of Transcendent Knowledge. Translated by Nalanda Translation Committee. Halifax, Nova Scotia: Nalanda Translation Committee.

Thrangu Rinpoche. *Distinguishing Dharma and Dharmata by Asanga and Maitreya with a Commentary by Thrangu Rinpoche, Geshe Lharamapa.* Translated by Jules B. Levinson. Boulder, Colo.: Namo Buddha Seminar, 1999.

———. *Distinguishing the Middle from the Extremes by Asanga and Maitreya: A Commentary by Thrangu Rinpoche, Geshe Lharamapa.* Translated by Jules B. Levinson. Boulder, Colo.: Namo Buddha Seminar, 2000.

———. *The Open Door to Emptiness.* Translated by Shakya Dorje. Boulder, Colo.: Namo Buddha Publications, 1997.

Trungpa, Chögyam. *Cutting through Spiritual Materialism.* Berkeley: Shambhala Publications, 1973.

———. *Dharma Art.* 1st ed. Boston: Shambhala Publications, 1996.

———. *The Heart of the Buddha.* 1st ed. Boston: Shambhala Publications, 1991.

———. *Training the Mind and Cultivating Loving-Kindness.* 1st ed. Boston: Shambhala Publications, 1993.

———. *Transcending Madness: The Experience of the Six Bardos.* 1st ed. Boston: Shambhala Publications, 1992.

Resources

For more information on the activities and teachings of Khenpo Tsültrim Gyamtso Rinpoche, please visit www.ktgrinpoche.org.

For more information on the activities and teachings of The Dzogchen Ponlop Rinpoche, please visit www.nalandabodhi.org and www.nitarthainstitute.org.

To find courses based on this book and other resources, please visit www.contemplatingreality.org.

Index

W HERE TITLES ARE cited as references only, they have generally not been indexed. Titles that are given special consideration are indexed in full. Appendix 1 is rich in textual references; only those titles that are given special consideration in the body of the book have been indexed. Key illustrations are listed under the sections "analogies," "examples," and "contemplations." Numbered groups are listed under their numbers—for example, "Two Charioteers" and "four noble truths."